The Insured Stock Purchase Agreement

with Sample Forms

Second Edition

Lawrence Brody
Stephen B. Daiker

Section of Real Property, Trust and Estate Law
American Bar Association

Cover design by ABA Publishing

ISBN 978-1-59031-875-1

11 10 09 08 5 4 3 2 1

Library of Congress Cataloging-in-Publication Data
Brody, Lawrence, 1942-
The insured stock purchase agreement with sample forms / Lawrence Brody, Stephen B. Daiker. — 2nd ed., rev. 2007.
    p. cm.
    Includes bibliographical references and index.
    1. Stock purchase agreements (Close corporations)—United States. 2. Insurance, Life—Law and legislation—United States. I. Daiker, Stephen B., 1965- II. Title.
KF1454.Z9B76 2007

346.73'0666—dc22   2007050735

Discounts are available for books ordered in bulk. Special consideration is given to state bars, CLE programs, and other bar-related organizations. Inquire at ABA Publishing, American Bar Association, 321 N. Clark Street, Chicago IL 60610.

Visit us at www.ababooks.org

Contents

About the Authors

Lawrence Brody is a partner of Bryan Cave LLP, an international law firm, resident in the St. Louis office. He is a member of its Private Client Service Group and its Technology, Entrepreneurial & Commercial Practice Client Service Group. He is an adjunct professor at Washington University School of Law, teaching estate planning and drafting, and a visiting adjunct professor at the University of Miami Law School, teaching a course on life insurance. He is the author or co-author of numerous articles and books on the use of life insurance in estate and employee benefit planning, including two BNA Tax Management Portfolios, two books for the National Underwriter Company, and a number of volumes in the ABA Insurance Counselor Series. Mr. Brody is a member of both the American College of Trust and Estate Counsel (ACTEC) and the American College of Tax Counsel and is a frequent participant at ALI-ABA programs and Society of Financial Professionals programs and teleconferences. He has spoken at all numerous life insurance industry programs (including the MDRT, the Top of the Table, AALU and the International Forum), many local estate planning council meetings, a number of state bar association conferences, and many national estate planning programs. He is a member of the Advisory Committee for the Philip E. Heckerling Institute on Estate Planning of the University of Miami School of Law, and is a member of the editorial boards of BNA's *Estates, Gifts, and Trusts Journal* and the Society of Financial Service Professionals *CLU Journal*. Mr. Brody received the designation of Accredited Estate Planner by the National Association of Estate Planners and Councils and was one of ten individuals awarded its Distinguished Accredited Estate Planner designation in the initial class in 2004.

Stephen B. Daiker is a partner of Bryan Cave LLP, St. Louis. He is a member of the Private Client Group and focuses his practice on sophisticated estate and gift tax planning for high networth individuals and families, and succession planning for owners of privately held businesses. He is a frequent speaker on these topics and has written articles for numerous publications, including *Taxation for Accountants, Taxation for Lawyers, The Florida Bar Journal, The Journal of the Missouri Bar, The Journal of Financial Planning* and *Tax Management Journal of Estates, Gifts and Trusts*. Mr. Daiker serves as a member of numerous local charitable boards, including the Endowment Council of the St. Louis Art Museum, the Gift Planning Committee of St. Louis Cardinal Glennon Children's Hospital, and the Gift on Bequest Council of Saint Louis University. He is a member of the bar associations of Florida and Missouri. He earned his bachelor's degree from Tulane University and his J.D. from St. Louis University.

About the Editors,
Insurance Counselor Series

William A. Drennan is an assistant professor with the Southern Illinois University School of Law. He teaches classes on federal income tax law, business tax law, trusts and estates, basic estate planning, and charities and charitable giving. He researches and writes in the areas of taxation and intellectual property. Prior to joining the faculty, Professor Drennan was in private practice and is currently of counsel to Husch & Eppenberger, LLC, in the tax and estate planning group. His experience includes extensive work in tax planning with life insurance, executive compensation, tax controversy work, estate planning, drafting of wills and trusts, and tax planning for charitable organizations. He is a member of the ABA sections of Taxation and Real Property, Trust and Estate Law, and is series editor for Trust and Estate Books/Media Committee, Insurance Counselor Series. He is also a member of the American Law Institute and the bar associations of Missouri and St. Louis. He is a fellow of the American College of Tax Counsel and the American College of Trust and Estate Counsel. He earned his J.D. from St. Louis University School of Law (magna cum laude) and an LL.M. in intellectual property from Washington University School of Law.

Michael G. Goldstein is senior vice president and counsel for the Newport Group, Inc., Newport Beach, California. He is an adjunct professor of law in the Graduate Tax Program of Washington University School of Law and has fellowships in the American Bar Foundation, American College of Tax Counsel, and American College of Trust and Estate Counsel. He has memberships in the American Law Institute and Association for Advanced Life Underwriting. He is also a member of the ABA's sections of Taxation, Real Property, Trust and Estate Law and is books editor for the Insurance Counselor Series, Executive Compensation and Insurance Committees. He was co-author and co-editor for *The Life Insurance Counselor: Taxation and Funding of Nonqualified Deferred Compensation—A Complete Guide to Design and Implementation*, and co-author of *Tax Management Portfolio Estate Planning for the Corporate Executive*. He earned a B.A. from Tulane University, a J.D. from the University of Missouri and an LL.M. (Taxation) from Washington University.

Acknowledgments

The first edition was authored by Lawrence Brody and Michael D. Weinberg. The authors of the first edition wish to thank both Douglas A. Rothermich, formerly an associate at Bryan Cave LLP, for his help in preparing an earlier version of these materials, and John Wood, then a summer clerk at Bryan Cave LLP, for his help in researching the state law surplus issues discussed in Chapter Four.

The authors of the second edition wish to thank Naomi Meisels, former counsel at Bryan Cave LLP, for her help in updating portions of these materials.

Authors' Note

The sample Shareholders Agreements and other forms included in this volume are provided for the reference of the drafting attorney as an educational aid in drafting a particular client's document(s). The authors and the publisher hereby expressly disclaim any liability for the use of any of the sample agreements, forms, or any of the other materials contained in this volume, and expressly state that no express or implied warranty is made as to the effectiveness, validity, or suitability of the forms or any other material contained herein for tax or legal purposes. The drafting lawyer is cautioned that the sample agreements, forms, and other materials contained herein have been prepared with an emphasis on general federal tax law in effect when these materials went to press; accordingly, they may not be appropriate to the state law requirements of any particular state, and because federal tax law changes constantly, a current knowledge of federal income and transfer tax law is required at the time a particular client's agreement is being planned and drafted. As always, the drafting lawyer is responsible for making all necessary modifications to the sample agreement(s) and other form(s) to make their use appropriate to the client's situation and to ensure compliance with both then-current federal tax law and applicable state law.

Introduction:
General Description of a Stock Purchase Agreement

A. General

A stock purchase agreement is a written contract among the corporation and its stockholders—or among the stockholders themselves. Typically, the stock purchase agreement will provide for the purchase of a stockholder's shares on the occurrence of various possible events, such as the stockholder's intent to transfer his or her shares during his or her lifetime, the purchase of the shares upon his or her total disability, upon his or her death, or other possible contingencies, sometimes called triggering events.

The purchase obligation of the corporation or the other stockholders at the death of a stockholder (or perhaps at the disability or retirement of the stockholder) under the stock purchase agreement is often funded (totally or partially) by an insurance policy (or policies) insuring the life of the selling stockholder. If such an "insured" stock purchase agreement is to be used, the insurance policy(ies) which will provide the purchase obligation funding should be owned by and payable to the purchaser(s) under the agreement—as described in Chapter One, the corporation or the other stockholders.

B. Purposes

Several different possible purposes can be accomplished by establishing a stock purchase agreement. One possible purpose is to protect the stockholders and the corporation against a stockholder transferring his or her shares—voluntarily or involuntarily—to an unwanted third party, thereby preserving control in the desired stockholder group. The use of a stock purchase agreement for this purpose can provide the corporation and/or all of the stockholders with the assurance that the stock will continue to be held among the existing stockholders—or permitted transferees—and will not be transferred to an unwanted third party.

A second possible purpose for establishing a stock purchase agreement is to provide each stockholder with a market for his or her shares on death, or in the event of the occurrence of certain lifetime contingencies (such as disability). The use of a stock purchase agreement for this purpose allows each stockholder (or his or her estate or the trustee of his or her revocable trust) to convert his or her illiquid stock interest into cash (or cash and the purchaser's notes).

A third possible purpose for a stock purchase agreement is to fix (to the extent possible) the value of a deceased stockholder's shares for death tax purposes at the price determined under the agreement, thereby preventing disputes over valuation with the Internal Revenue Service and avoiding the increased death taxes that could result from an increased valuation. Being unable to fix estate tax values at the agreed price could put the deceased stockholder's estate in the difficult position of paying tax on a value that exceeds the amount the estate received for the shares, or even paying a tax tha exceeds the consideration received for the shares. In addition, if that were the case, the issue of who would bear the increased tax—the purchaser or the decedent's residuary beneficiaries—must be considered and planned for; that will be determined not by the stock purchase agreement, but by the deceased stockholder's Will or Revocable Trust (in the applicable tax apportionment clause). The impact of Section 2703—a part of I.R.C. Chapter 14, added by the Omnibus Budget Reconciliation Act of 1990—on this issue for family businesses is discussed in Chapter Six.

A fourth possible purpose for establishing a stock purchase agreement (which may be a subset of the first purpose described above) is to prevent a transfer of stock in an S Corporation to an ineligible stockholder or to prevent a transferee of stock in such a corporation from terminating the S Corporation election. Under the Subchapter S Revision Act of 1982, an S Corporation election can be voluntarily revoked by stockholders holding more than one-half of the stock, under Section 1362(d), and will be involuntarily revoked by a transfer of stock to an ineligible stockholder, under Section 1361(b). The relaxation of the eligible shareholder rules for S Corporations by the 1996 and 2004 legislation described in Chapter Nine may make this issue somewhat less important in the future. Special concerns in planning stock purchase agreements in S Corporations are also discussed in Chapter Nine.

Obviously, in any specific stock purchase agreement, only some of these general purposes may be applicable.

Chapter One

Forms of Stock Purchase Agreements

A stock purchase agreement may take several different forms. The principal distinction between the different forms is which party (e.g., the corporation or the other stockholders) will have the right or obligation to purchase a stockholder's stock upon the occurrence of a triggering event. As discussed in the Introduction, the triggering event in a stock purchase agreement might be the stockholder's death, disability, or some other occurrence specified in the agreement.

A. Stock Redemption

A stock redemption agreement is an agreement among the corporation and the stockholders. In a stock redemption arrangement, the corporation (as the party obligated to purchase its own stock) will effect the purchase of the shares at the death of a stockholder, or on the occurrence of some other event specified in the agreement. The corporation will use its own funds to satisfy its purchase obligation under the stock redemption agreement.

In an insured stock redemption arrangement, the corporation will own one insurance policy on the life of each stockholder. Upon the death of a stockholder, the corporation will collect the proceeds of the insurance policy on his or her life and use those funds to satisfy its purchase obligation for the deceased stockholder's shares under the redemption agreement. The insurance will be owned by and payable to the corporation, and the corporation will pay the premiums due on the insurance policies insuring the lives of the stockholders.

B. Cross-Purchase

A cross-purchase agreement is an agreement among the stockholders only; the corporation does not need to be a party to the agreement (but is, in most cases). In a cross-purchase agreement, the remaining (or surviving) stockholder(s) effect the purchase of the withdrawing or deceased stockholder's shares themselves, and each purchasing stockholder will use his or her own funds to satisfy this purchase obligation.

In an insured cross-purchase arrangement, each stockholder will be the owner and beneficiary of an insurance policy on the lives of the other stockholders; the policies are described as being cross-owned. As discussed in Chapter Five, unless a split-dollar or loan arrangement is used to allow the corporation to bear all of (or at least a substantial part of) the insurance premiums, each stockholder will pay the premiums on the insurance he or she owns on the lives of the other stockholder(s) out of his or her after-tax funds.

C. Combination

In a combination stock purchase agreement, the stock redemption and cross-purchase attributes are combined. For example, the corporation might have the first option to purchase the shares of a stockholder who wants to sell his or her stock during life, with the remaining stockholders being granted successive options to purchase the shares not acquired by the corporation. Alternatively, the order of the successive options might be reversed.

As another alternative, upon the death of a stockholder the corporation could be the required purchaser of the deceased stockholder's shares up to the Section 303 dollar limit (discussed in Chapter Eight, section C), with the other stockholders required to purchase the balance of the decedent's shares. Life insurance funding in this situation may be difficult to arrange because of the uncertainty regarding the number of shares that can be redeemed under Section 303. As discussed in Chapter Eight, this amount will generally be equal to the amount of federal and state death taxes due on the deceased stockholder's estate.

Life insurance funding for a combination agreement may also be difficult to arrange, since it is unclear which party will be the purchaser and, therefore, which party will need the insurance proceeds to fund the purchase. However, fewer problems generally will be encountered in "switching" the insurance funding from a cross-purchase to a redemption plan than vice-versa. Going from a redemption to a cross-purchase plan will involve transferring corporate-owned policies to the stockholders on a cross-owned basis. This transfer will raise compensation or dividend issues and could create a transfer-for-value issue under Section 101(a)(2). As discussed in detail later in this chapter, if the transfer of an insurance policy from the corporation to the stockholders is a transfer for value, this will result in a loss of at least some of the income tax exemption that is otherwise available under Section 101(a) on collection of the death proceeds. On the other hand, going from a cross-purchase to a redemption arrangement will require transferring policies that are cross-owned by the shareholders to the corporation. Those transfers should be income-tax free and should not raise transfer-for-value issues (transfers to a corporation in which the insureds are stockholders are exempt for transfer-for-value purposes).

D. The Wait-and-See Buy-Sell

In this type of agreement (developed by Stephan R. Leimberg and Morrie Rosenbloom), the decision on the identity of the purchaser—whether the corporation or the other stockholders—is not required to be made until the triggering event occurs, and is presumably based on which purchaser then makes the most sense, from both a tax and a non-tax point of view.

The same life insurance funding issue is presented in this type of arrangement, and again, cross-purchase funding probably makes sense, for the same reasons discussed in section C, above.

E. Advantages and Disadvantages of Each When Life Insurance Funding Is Used

When the agreement is to be funded with life insurance and there are a large number of stockholders, a redemption arrangement may be administratively advantageous, because if a cross-purchase agreement is funded with insurance on the life of each stockholder, the number of policies required to fully fund the agreement could become unmanageable. In the absence of the special planning discussed below, the number of policies required would be determined using the formula n(n-1).

For example, if 10 stockholders with equal stockholdings are parties to a cross-purchase agreement, 90 policies [10 x (10-1)] are required to fully fund the agreement. The insured cross-purchase agreement will be fully funded if, upon the death of any stockholder, each of the other nine stockholders receives insurance proceeds sufficient to purchase one-ninth of the deceased stockholder's shares (as well as the insurance owned by the deceased stockholder on the lives of the other survivors). Because it is uncertain which stockholder will die first, each stockholder must own a policy on all nine other stockholders.

In addition to the administrative issue of purchasing a large number of initial policies, at the death of a stockholder who is a party to a cross-purchase agreement, the policies that he or she owned on the lives of the survivors (now owned by the deceased stockholder's estate or revocable trust) will need to be transferred to the remaining stockholders (who will purchase them for their respective values on a cross-owned basis), in order to continue full funding under a cross-owned arrangement. Therefore, the transfer-for-value issue in any such transfer must be considered, since the policies are being purchased by the non-insured stockholders for cash. Accordingly, absent special planning, the policy proceeds will lose some part of their income tax exclusion under Section 101(a), unless the transferees are otherwise exempt for purposes of this transfer-for-value rule. Interestingly, co-stockholders are *not* exempt transferees under this rule, but partners of the insured in a partnership (and members with the insured in a limited liability corporation (LLC) taxed as a partnership) are exempt transferees.

One possible solution to this transfer-for-value problem associated with a cross-purchase agreement between more than two stockholders could be to have the stockholders form a state law valid partnership, or an LLC treated as a partnership for federal income tax purposes (even if the partnership or LLC has nothing to do with the insurance, such as owning investments or other business interests). The creation of a state law valid partnership or such an LLC by the stockholders will make each of them exempt transferees for transfer-for-value purposes when they purchase policies on one another's lives from the estate or revocable trust of the deceased stockholder (as they would be partners of the insureds). *See, e.g.,* Ltr. Ruls. 9042023, 9235029, and 9239033. In addition to solving the transfer-for-value problem, such a partnership or LLC could also solve the administrative problem of the large number of policies required to fully fund the arrangement. Specifically, the partnership or LLC could own one policy on each stockholder; at each death, the partnership or LLC would collect the proceeds and distribute them to the survivors, and the decedent's estate or revocable trust would sell its stock in the corporation to the survivors.

Ltr. Rul. 9309021 apparently approved for this purpose a partnership, the only stated purpose of which was to own and "manage" policies transferred from the corporation in connection with a switch from a redemption to a cross-purchase arrangement. It is not clear that such a partnership would be respected for income tax purposes, after issuance of the so-called partnership "anti-abuse" rules of Reg. Sec. 1.701-2. *See also* Rev. Proc. 96-12, 1996-1 C.B. 616, stating the Internal Revenue Service's no-ruling policy on a partnership for transfer-for-value purposes where substantially all of its assets consist of insurance on the partners' lives, Ltr. Rul. 9239033, in which the Service expressed no opinion on whether the entity would be classified as a partnership for tax purposes, and Ltr. Rul. 9843024, warning that the Service would not rule on the insured's status as a partner if his or her interest were reduced or the partnership disposed of its non-insurance assets. *See also* Ltr. Rul. 9410039, holding that admission and withdrawal of a partner is not a transfer for value of the underlying partnership-owned policies, as long as the partnership does not terminate as a result of the admitted or withdrawn partner, and Ltr . Rul. 9625013, in which the Service held that transfers of policies among members of an LLC that was taxed as a partnership would also be treated as exempt transfers under this exception, allowing the use of such an LLC as an alternative to a partnership in this situation.

As an alternative, where the cross-purchase format is utilized, the stockholders could form a state law valid partnership (or an LLC taxed as a partnership) that would both hold their shares and acquire a single policy on each of their lives (owned by and payable to the partnership or LLC). At the death of a stockholder, the partnership (or the LLC) would collect the death proceeds of the policy on the deceased stockholder's life and exchange the policy proceeds for the deceased stockholder's shares in the corporation and his or her interest in the entity. This avoids both the problems associated with the large number of policies required for a standard cross-purchase agreement and the transfer-for-value issue at each stockholder's death. *See Estate of Tompkins v. Commissioner*, 13 T.C. 1054 (1949), and *Estate of Mitchell v. Commissioner*, 37 B.T.A. 1 (1938), suggesting that neither the value of the stock nor the insurance proceeds used to fund the stock purchase will be included in the deceased stockholder's gross estate for the estate tax purposes (although the value of the decedent's partnership interest would be included).

This use of a partnership (or an LLC taxed as a partnership) to own the stock as well as the insurance as an alternative to the standard cross-purchase agreement is not, however, available if the corporation is an S Corporation because, even after the recent legislation relaxing some of the restrictions on the ownership of S Corporation shares, neither a partnership nor an LLC can own S Corporation stock. Section 1361(b)(1)(B). However, as noted above, the partnership or LLC could own one policy on the life of each stockholder (assuming that would be enough to validate the entity for state law purposes), collect the death proceeds, and distribute them to the surviving stockholders, allowing them to personally purchase the decedent's shares and his or her interest in the entity.

Because of the potential transfer-for-value issue raised by a cross-purchase agreement, a partnership (or an LLC taxed as a partnership) rather than a trust (which is sometimes suggested) should be used as the entity owning the insurance, since the cross-purchase technique appears to involve transfers of interests in the policies at each death, and transfers of interests in policies among partners are exempt from the transfer-for-value rule of Section 101(a)(2). Ltr. Ruls. 9042023, 9235029, 9239033, and especially 9309021. *See also* Ltr. Rul. 9328010, in which the stockholders combined the use of multiple partnerships and trusts to transfer a policy of insurance on each stockholder's life from the corporation to several different trusts for the purpose of purchasing the stockholder's stock, effectively converting the stockholders' agreement from a redemption agreement to a cross-purchase agreement, without any adverse transfer-for-value or double estate tax inclusion problems. *See* Brody & Leimberg, *The Not So Tender Trap; The Transfer for Value Rule—Revisited*, 32 ESTATE PLANNING 10 (Oct.-Nov. 2005), for a full discussion of these issues.

On the other hand, there are some disadvantages to using a redemption agreement funded with life insurance. In the first place, the policies insuring the lives of the stockholders will be owned by the corporation, subjecting them to corporate creditors on an ongoing basis. In addition, and more important, the insurance proceeds themselves, when collected by the corporation, will be corporate assets for all purposes, including availability to corporate creditors; as discussed below, this is a critical issue to negotiate with current (and future) secured creditors, to be sure the proceeds can be used as intended to carry out the redemption.

The insurance proceeds will also increase the value of the corporation at the death of a stockholder, and, because those insurance proceeds (in excess of the cash values) will not have been carried on the books of the corporation, an adjustment to the purchase price of the corporation for such excess proceeds should be considered where the agreed price was based on some variation of book value. However, note that (as discussed below) this adjustment will cause the arrangement to be underfunded. In addition, those proceeds will likely affect the valuation of the corporation for estate tax purposes (although, depending on the valuation method used, perhaps not on a dollar-for-dollar basis), unless the stock purchase agreement ignores them or the valuation technique used to value the shares does not take them into account. In either case, disregarding the proceeds for valuation purposes is an economic issue for the parties to consider and (as discussed in Chapter Six) is also potentially a Section 2703 issue when family members are involved, although the circuit court decision in the *Blount* case, discussed in Chapter Six, upheld disregarding those proceeds in valuing the corporation, even under Section 2703.

Section 264(a)(4) restricts the deductibility of interest on corporate-owned policies to the interest on loans not in excess of $50,000 per insured, with additional limits on the number of insureds and the amount of interest deductible imposed by the provisions of the Health Insurance Portability Act and Accountability of 1996 (HIPAA). Finally, the Section 163(d) interest classification rules will prohibit the deductibility of interest paid on indebtedness on policies owned by the stockholders in a cross-purchase arrangement, as it will be considered personal interest.

For C Corporations, the increase in the cash surrender value in excess of premiums and the death proceeds in excess of cash values are subject to the adjusted current earnings preference for years beginning after 1989. Sections 56(f) and (g), added by TRA 86. As discussed in Chapter Eight, section F, this may result in a 15% penalty tax on those excess proceeds in the year of the insured's death, depending on the corporation's regular tax-AMT posture. As further discussed in Chapter Eight, section F, the provision of the Revenue Reconciliation Act of 1989 allowing a carry-forward of any AMT generated by this preference against future regular corporate tax and the provisions of the 1997 Act exempting "small" business entities (those with less than $5 million in gross receipts) from this tax should help to alleviate this concern for many otherwise affected corporations.

Finally, the amendments to Section 101 made by the COLI Best Practices Act provisions of the Pension Protection Act of 2006 could, in some cases, cause a portion of the death proceeds of insurance designated to fund a corporation's redemption obligations to be included in the corporation's income. *See* Section 101(j). However, it is likely that, in most closely held corporations, this provision would not be an issue, as the insureds will meet the eligibility requirements of that Section; however, compliance with the prior notice and consent, record-keeping, and reporting provisions of that Section also will be required.

F. Other Tax Differences between the Forms

Under a cross-purchase agreement, the survivors' bases for the stock acquired from the estate of a deceased stockholder will be the price paid for the shares, but in a redemption arrangement, the surviving stockholders' bases in their shares will not change. This is an important advantage of a cross-purchase arrangement, especially if the surviving stockholders plan to sell their shares during life. As noted in Chapters Seven and Nine, in an S Corporation, there will normally be at least a partial step-up in basis of the shares of the remaining stockholders in a life insurance-funded redemption arrangement, reducing the importance of this difference; however, because a proportionate part of the insurance death proceeds received by the S Corporation will be attributable to the shares of the decedent (which were stepped up to fair market value at death under Section 1014), that part of the basis step-up resulting from the income tax-free receipt of the death proceeds by the corporation will be "wasted." A possible solution to the wasted basis problem in some circumstances is discussed in Chapter 9, Section B.

Another tax consideration is the interest classification rules of Section 163 on both the interest paid by the stockholders on financed cross-owned policies and the interest paid by them on any permitted deferred payment of the non-insured purchase price. The interest on the deferred payments might be considered investment (rather than trade or business) interest with limited deductibility; the interest on policy loans might be so considered or might be classified as personal interest, with no deductibility.

Finally, as discussed in detail in Chapters Seven and Nine, the income tax consequences of each type of arrangement (which may be different for the seller, especially in a family-owned corporation) must be analyzed.

G. Non-Tax Considerations in Choosing between the Forms

If a cross-purchase agreement is used when the stockholders' ages, percentage interests in the corporation, or financial abilities are very different, the younger, less wealthy stockholder will be at a disadvantage in trying to purchase insurance to fund or assume the obligation for the purchase of the older, wealthier stockholders' interests in the corporation. As discussed in Chapter Five, a split-dollar or loan arrangement in which the corporation pays all (or most) of the premiums may help "equalize" the funding obligations of the stockholders.

In addition, because in a redemption agreement the corporation is the purchaser, the proportion of each remaining stockholder's interest in the corporation will remain the same relative to the other remaining stockholders both before and after the redemption, but the absolute percentage interest of each remaining stockholder in the corporation will, of course, increase. For example, if three stockholders each own one-third of a corporation, at the first death (and the redemption of the deceased stockholder's stock), the two surviving stockholders will each then own one-half of the corporation— but each will still own the same percentage interest as his or her co-stockholder. This is an important issue to consider where there are minority stockholders; as an alternative, a cross-purchase arrangement among only the majority stockholders could be used.

Finally, in a redemption arrangement, both state corporate law and any loan or other restriction on the repurchase of shares by the corporation itself must be considered. Some state corporate laws restrict redemptions to those made out of "surplus"; whether insurance funding would create such surplus depends on state law. See Chapter Four. In addition, as noted above, the rights of creditors to the death proceeds and, therefore, their availability to carry out the redemption may need to be negotiated with existing secured creditors in advance (and with new secured creditors as they arise).

A Comparison Table highlighting many of the distinctions between stock redemption agreements and cross-purchase agreements is set forth in Exhibit 1.

Chapter Two

Possible Types of Restrictions on Stock and the Events Permitting or Requiring the Purchase of a Stockholder's Stock

A. Types of Restrictions on Stock

As noted in the Introduction, the primary motivations for establishing a stockholders' agreement include: (i) providing each stockholder with assurance that the shares held by other stockholders will not be transferred to an unwanted third party, and/or (ii) providing each stockholder with the knowledge that upon the occurrence of a triggering event (i.e., death, disability, cessation of employment, etc.), there will be a "market" and, in at least some cases, a known price for his or her shares. The transfer restrictions or purchase requirements imposed by a stockholders' agreement will be designed to accomplish one or both of these objectives.

Stockholders' agreements may impose several different types of transfer restrictions or purchase requirements on the underlying stock; however, they will ordinarily fall into one of the following four categories:

1. Transfers are allowed, but only to one or more defined "permitted transferees."
2. Other transfers are permitted but will be subject to a right of first refusal by the other stockholders or the corporation (or both).
3. The corporation or the other stockholders will have an option to purchase the shares upon the occurrence of a triggering event.
4. Transfers are mandatory upon the occurrence of a triggering event.

An absolute prohibition against transfer is one type of restriction that could be placed on stock; however, such a restriction may be invalid, if it is unlimited in time. The general rule is that a reasonable restriction—unlike an absolute prohibition on transfer—will be enforceable if it is entered into freely between the parties. *See, e.g., Bloomingdale v. Bloomingdale*, 177 N.Y. Supp. 873 (Sup. Ct. 1919). One commentator has summarized what constitutes a "reasonable restriction" as follows:

Factors which courts have considered, in the absence of a controlling statute, in determining whether restrictions are reasonable include the following: the size of the corporation, the degree of restraint on the power to alienate, the length of time the restriction is to remain in effect, the method to be used in determining the transfer or option price of shares subject to the restraint, the fairness or unfairness of the procedure used to adopt a restriction, the likelihood of its contributing to the attainment of corporate objectives, the possibility that a hostile shareholder would seriously injure the corporation, and the likelihood that the restriction will promote the best interests of the enterprise as a whole. The underlying test has been whether the restraint is sufficiently needed by the particular enterprise to justify overriding the general policy against restraints on alienation.

F. O'Neal & R. Thompson, *O'Neal's Close Corporation* § 7.7 (3d Revised Edition, 1997).

An alternative to an absolute prohibition on transfer could be to prohibit transfers generally, but to allow transfers to a permitted group without first having to obtain the consent of the corporation or the other shareholders. The group of "permitted transferees" of stock might include the other stockholders, the stockholder's family, or the trustee(s) of a revocable living trust created by the stockholder. Additionally, the restriction might simply be in the form of a right of first refusal, under which the corporation and/or the other stockholders have the first right to buy if a stockholder wishes to sell his or her shares during life. By allowing the corporation and/or the other stockholders a right of first refusal, the stockholder wishing to sell his or her shares is free to seek the best offer he or she can negotiate, but the corporation and/or the other shareholders will have the right to match that best offer for a specified period of time (e.g., for 60 days following receipt of notice from the selling shareholder of the offer received). From the selling shareholder's view, the potential problem with rights of first refusal is that it is likely to be difficult or impossible to negotiate a fair purchase with an outsider if the buyer believes that the corporation and/or the other stockholders will simply exercise their option to "buy the shares away" from him or her.

Another form of restriction is an option under which the corporation or the other stockholders have the right to buy—to "call"—the shares upon the occurrence of a triggering event. This is similar to a right of first refusal, since once a stockholder indicates an intention to sell his or her shares, the corporation or the other stockholders are given an option to buy. However, unlike a right of first refusal, the use of an option can provide greater flexibility for the corporation and/or other stockholders if the triggering events under the agreement include, for example, the filing of a bankruptcy or divorce by or against a stockholder or termination of employment, in addition to a voluntary transfer by a selling stockholder.

In certain situations, it might be desirable for each of the stockholders to have the right to sell—to "put" their shares to the corporation. For example, the use of a put option may be desirable when there will be sufficient liquidity in the corporation, and each of the stockholders would like to have the right (but not the obligation) to "cash-out" at retirement, disability, or upon their death. However, if multiple shareholders "put" their shares over a relatively short period of time, the corporation's finances may be strained.

The restrictions imposed by the stockholders' agreement could also be a mandatory purchase by the corporation or the other stockholders. If a mandatory purchase is included in the stockholders' agreement, then, for example, upon the death of a stockholder, the deceased stockholder's estate (or the trustee of his or her revocable trust) must sell, and the corporation or the other stockholders must purchase, the shares of stock formerly held by the deceased stockholder. A mandatory purchase may also be imposed by the stockholders' agreement upon the occurrence of a disability or termination of the stockholder's employment with the corporation. As discussed in Chapter Five, these purchase obligations will be more difficult to fund with insurance.

Although the purchase obligation will be mandatory, the use of this type of restriction can still provide some flexibility for the other stockholders. For example, upon the occurrence of a triggering event, the other stockholders could have the option to purchase the shares; however, if they do not purchase all of the shares, then the corporation must redeem the balance of the shares. The potential problem (or opportunity) with this alternative is that it could result in the wealthier stockholders being able to gain greater control over the corporation upon the occurrence of a triggering event if the other stockholders cannot afford to exercise their purchase options at that time.

Although there are several ways in which these four basic restrictions can be combined, perhaps the most common set of restrictions is:

1. No transfer of shares by a stockholder during life is permitted, except perhaps to permitted defined transferees, unless the corporation or the other stockholders consent; in an S Corporation, consent is required for any proposed transfer, and any purported transfer in violation of the agreement is void, to ensure qualification of the transferee as an eligible S Corporation stockholder.
2. If a stockholder wishes to transfer his or her stock during life to a person not permitted or consented to, the corporation or the other stockholders have a right of first refusal to buy the shares; if an involuntary transfer of the shares (such as in a dissolution of marriage) is threatened or takes place, the corporation or the other stockholders (or in some cases the divorcing stockholder) have a similar right of first refusal.
3. At the death of a stockholder, a mandatory purchase of his or her stock by the corporation or the other stockholders is required. Alternatively, the corporation or the other stockholders might have an option (a call) to acquire those shares, leaving them with the flexibility to decide at that time if the deceased stockholder's transferee is a "desirable" stockholder.

Again, loan (or other) agreements to which the corporation is a party may contain restrictions on the repurchase by a corporation of its stock. A waiver of this provision should be obtained from the lender or other party to the agreement at the time the stock redemption agreement is adopted (or when such agreements are entered into).

B. Events Permitting or Requiring the Purchase of a Stockholder's Stock

As indicated above, there are several different events that can trigger the obligation to purchase or sell under the stockholders' agreement. Any of the following events (or any combination of them) may be used as triggering events:

(1) *A Stockholder's Intent to Transfer His or Her Stock During Life.* The stockholders' agreement may provide that any stockholder's attempt to transfer his or her shares will trigger a permitted or required purchase right in the corporation and/or other stockholders. Com-

monly, a right of first refusal in the corporation and/or the other stockholders is provided, allowing them to match an outside offer. If the corporation and/or other stockholders choose not to exercise this right of first refusal, then the selling stockholder is free to transfer his or her shares to whomever he or she wishes.

    Administratively, the stockholders' agreement might provide that if a stockholder wants to transfer his or her shares to a third party, the transferring stockholder will have to provide the corporation and/or the other stockholders with notice of his or her intent to transfer the shares. This notice will usually serve as the triggering event that gives rise to the corporation's and/or other stockholders' right(s) of first refusal.

    Again, the existence of such a right will have the practical effect of making it difficult for a stockholder to negotiate a sale to an outsider.

(2) *Involuntary Sale or Transfer of a Stockholder's Stock,* such as to satisfy a judgment, at a bankruptcy sale, or in a marriage dissolution. To avoid the risk that shares of the corporation's stock will be transferred to an unwanted third party, the corporation or the other stockholders are normally given the option to purchase the shares from the transferee (or, more commonly, from the proposed transferor prior to the transfer) when the transfer is involuntary. An involuntary transferee could include a judgment creditor of a stockholder, a stockholder's trustee in bankruptcy, or the spouse of a stockholder in a marriage dissolution proceeding. In any of these situations, unless the affected stockholder (as opposed to the corporation or all of the stockholders pro rata) has the first option to purchase the shares, his or her percentage interest in the corporation will be reduced. If the affected stockholder had that option, he or she could retain the shares and give the involuntary transferee the value of the shares (if the funds were available to do so).

    Clearly, the interest of any such third parties may be adverse to that of the other stockholders, if (as is usual) profits are routinely reinvested in the business to build further corporate growth. An involuntary transferee may desire to have cash for the shares, or at least to have the corporate earnings distributed. The option to purchase or requirement to sell shares in this context will avoid disputes between the existing stockholders and the involuntary transferee and will provide a means of assuring continuity of management for the corporation.

    The use of a purchase option or requirement triggered upon an involuntary transfer is protective in nature for the corporation and the existing stockholders. Accordingly, a lower price might be (and normally is) used upon the occurrence of this type of triggering event than the price that will be used in connection with a voluntary transfer or a transfer at death. In fact, since there is no economic incentive to provide such a transferee with full value for the shares being involuntarily transferred, there is always a risk that too low a price would be held to be invalid and could therefore be disregarded.

(3) *Termination of a Stockholder's Employment.* In a closely held corporation, the stockholders may intend that the corporation continue to be owned by those who are active in the business. When retention of stock ownership within a defined group is intended, an option to purchase is usually given to the corporation and/or the other stockholders on termination of a stockholder-employee's employment by the corporation.

    For a minority stockholder, once he or she is no longer employed by the corporation, the value of his or her stock could, as a practical matter, become worthless—he or she would have little or no control over how corporate earnings are distributed, and without an ongoing employment relationship, there would be no economic benefit to continued stock ownership (except in the case of a later sale of the corporation). To protect a minority stockholder-employee, a mandatory purchase is often required upon the termination of his or her employment—or the stockholders' agreement could provide the stockholder-employee with a put option that could be exercised within a specified period upon termination of employment. The same considerations may be present when a stockholder voluntarily terminates his or her employment (such as at retirement). Negotiating retirement buyouts can be difficult—an automatic buyout at retirement may encourage employees to retire, and funding such a buyout may be difficult.

(4) *Death of a Stockholder.* Commonly, a purchase of a deceased stockholder's shares is required at death by the corporation and/or other stockholders. When the stockholders' agreement provides for a purchase obligation at death, it may be funded with life insurance on the life of the stockholder, as discussed in Chapter Five. As an alternative to a mandatory purchase at death, a put may be given to the estate (or other transferee), or a call may be given to the corporation and/or the other stockholders. As discussed in Chapter Six, that alternative might make sense in a family corporation because of Section 2703.

(5) *Disability of a Stockholder.* It is possible (although not common) to make the permanent and total disability of a stockholder for a specified period of time (however that is defined) an event either requiring the purchase of the disabled stockholder's shares or giving the disabled stockholder a put, which would allow him or her to require the repurchase of his or her shares. Note the difficult definitional problems in determining whether disability has occurred, as well as the issue of how (if at all) to treat recovery from what was perceived as a "permanent" disability.

Chapter Three

Methods of Determining Purchase Price under the Agreement

Regardless of whether the stock purchase agreement is drafted as a redemption agreement or a cross-purchase agreement, the agreement should include a "purchase price" (or at least a method or formula for arriving at a price)—that is, the price at which the stock subject to the agreement will be purchased upon the occurrence of a triggering event (e.g., the death of a stockholder) or, when the parties are not merely matching a third-party purchase price, under a right of first refusal. There are several different methods that might be used to determine the purchase price under a stockholders' agreement.

The method used for determining the purchase price can provide for a fixed price specified in the agreement. For example, the price could be stated as the book value per share or some other agreed-upon value. As an alternative to using a fixed price amount, the stock purchase agreement could provide that upon the occurrence of a triggering event, the stock will be purchased at its then appraised value, or at a price determined by the use of a formula provided in the agreement.

Although there is no right or wrong method for determining the purchase price, the method selected should provide the parties to the stock purchase agreement with the purchase price that meets their objectives. If the parties intend that, upon the occurrence of a triggering event, the stock purchase agreement will provide for the purchase of the stock at its then fair market value, the agreement should use a method that will reflect increases or decreases in that value from the date of the agreement. If the parties plan to use life insurance as a means of funding the purchase obligation upon the occurrence of a triggering event, then a method should be selected that will provide for a fixed amount—possibly subject to adjustment as the parties may agree from time to time. For closely held stock that is subject to a stock purchase agreement between family members, the method selected should provide for a price that represents the fair market value of the stock to avoid any concerns associated with the application of Section 2703. Section 2703 and its impact on planning and drafting agreements for family-owned corporations are discussed in Chapter Six.

The most usual methods for determining the purchase price under a stock purchase agreement are discussed below.

A. Book Value

When a stock purchase agreement provides that the stock will be purchased at book value upon the occurrence of a triggering event, the price per share of stock is determined simply by referring to the company's financial statements. For example, if the corporation has only one class of stock and there is no paid-in capital or treasury stock, the book value per share will be determined by subtracting the liabilities from the assets and dividing this difference by the number of outstanding shares.

The advantage associated with the book value method of determining the purchase price is that the price can be determined quickly and easily, without any significant expense. Additionally, if insurance will be used to fund the purchase obligation, the corporation's periodic financial statements provide a ready reference to determine if the amount of insurance carried is still appropriate. However, as book value is based on historic depreciated values, this method does not take into consideration market appreciation or depreciation in asset values, earnings capability, or the value of the corporation's goodwill. Accordingly, the "pure" book value per share does not usually represent the true value of the stock.

One alternative to the "pure" book value method is the use of a "modified book value." *Modified book value* adjusts book value to take into account the fair market value of assets that have a more or less readily determinable value, such as investment securities or real estate. Also, the excess of the death proceeds of corporate-owned insurance over booked cash values may be a modification to book value. This method of determining the purchase price under a stock purchase agreement retains most of the advantages associated with the book value method (relative simplicity, without significant costs or delays in determining the price) but more accurately reflects the true value of the stock—although it also does not adjust for the corporation's earning capacity, its goodwill, or its going-concern value, and does not include a discount for lack of control or lack of marketability.

In the case of a family-owned corporation, either book value method may cause problems under Section 2703, because the purchase price under the agreement may fail to establish the value of the stock for estate tax purposes, as described in Chapter Six.

B. Agreed Value

Under this method, the stock purchase agreement provides that the purchase price per share will be agreed upon by the parties to the agreement. The theory of using this method is that the stockholders are best able to value their own business. In addition, this method is arguably fair, at least among unrelated parties, as no individual stockholder knows whether he or she will be required to buy or sell. As with the book value method, this method provides the parties to the agreement with the purchase price without any costly appraisals or time delays upon the occurrence of a triggering event.

This method is particularly attractive when life insurance will be used to fund the purchase obligation under the stock purchase agreement, because the amount required to fund the purchase obligation is a known value. However, periodic evaluation (or some other adjustment to the agreed value) is necessary to prevent the value from becoming "stale" and for the agreement to remain equitable. Although this is probably the most frequently used arrangement, as discussed in Chapter Six, it could pose a problem in a family-held corporation when Section 2703 applies to the agreement.

C. Appraised Value

This method provides that upon the occurrence of a triggering event, the stock will be appraised and the appraised value of the stock will set the purchase price for purposes of the stock purchase agreement. This may provide the most accurate valuation of the stock's fair market value, but the problem of finding qualified appraisers and the inevitable expense and delay of obtaining the appraisal are deterrents to the use of this method.

In a closely held corporation when the stock purchase agreement is between family members, use of this method avoids the risk that Section 2703 will impose a higher value on the stock for transfer-tax purposes. The appraised value of the stock will usually be the best evidence of fair market value. By its terms, Section 2703 does not apply to transfers of stock at fair market value (determined without regard to the restrictions imposed by the agreement). See Chapter Six for a more detailed discussion of the application of Section 2703 to stock purchase agreements in family businesses.

D. Use of a Formula

The use of a formula valuation to determine the price in a stock purchase agreement is intended to ensure that the price under the agreement will represent the fair value of the stock at any point in time. The stock purchase agreement could provide that upon the occurrence of a triggering event, the price will be determined by the formula the parties to the agreement believe is most reflective of fair market value. For example, if the parties believe that fair market value is best determined by multiplying the corporate after-tax earnings by a specific factor, this formula could be used in the stock purchase agreement.

With the formula method for determining the price, some capitalized amount is usually used, such as net earnings, net revenues, or net cash flow. If a capitalized net earnings formula is used, average earnings over a representative period are capitalized at a multiple corresponding to the risk inherent in the business. Similarly, with capitalized net revenues or cash flow, these amounts would be multiplied by a specific factor to determine the value of the corporation.

The difficulties with this method are in determining a representative period and a suitable multiple as a capitalization factor. The appropriate capitalization factor is often determined by sampling publicly traded companies of similar size and in the same industry (if there are such public companies) to determine what capitalization amount results in the market value of these companies.

E. A Combination of Methods

In addition to the four basic methods for determining a price under a stock purchase agreement, any two or more of the four basic methods can be combined in a variety of ways.

A common way of combining these different methods is to use an agreed value plus an adjustment for interim increases or decreases in book value since the date of the last agreed valuation. Such a combination of methods can provide for a price that includes a value for the corporation's goodwill or going-concern value (as part of the agreed value amount), as well as appropriate adjustments to reflect the changes in value during the financial reporting periods following the agreement on value.

The Internal Revenue Service has used a formula that combines both book value and capitalization of earnings approaches in its published rulings on valuing the shares of closely held corporations. Rev. Rul. 68-609, 1968-2 C.B. 327, *superseding and restating* A.R.M. 34, 2 C.B. 31 (1920), *as modified by* A.R.M. 68, 3 C.B. 43 (1920).

F. Using More Than One Method

A stock purchase agreement could also use a mixture of methods for determining the price, using one method for one triggering event and another method for a different triggering event. For example, the stock purchase agreement might provide for the use of an agreed value at the death of a stockholder and the use of an adjusted book value for voluntary or involuntary lifetime sales. By mixing the method for determining the price in this manner, the stockholders' agreement could provide real value to a decedent's heirs but penalize a stockholder who wants to get out early or a transferee in an involuntary sale, such as a trustee in bankruptcy (although, as discussed in Chapter Two, a discrepancy between the price payable under the agreement for different triggering events always raises the possibility that a purchase at the lower price will be challenged as being other than arm's length and, therefore, not binding on the proposed transferee).

G. The Extent to Which Life Insurance Should Be Reflected in the Purchase Price

Regardless of which valuation method is used, the issue of the fairness of taking the insurance cash values or death proceeds into account should be considered. In computing the purchase price payable under a stock redemption agreement for a lifetime redemption, the cash values of funding insurance policies will usually be included; if any excess of premiums paid over cash values is also included, a selling stockholder will be repaid his or her entire proportionate share of premiums paid by the corporation for the insurance. However, life insurance death proceeds (in excess of cash values) are generally not added to the purchase price determined at the death of a stockholder under a stock redemption arrangement; otherwise, the price payable for the deceased stockholder's stock will, in most cases, be underfunded.

> Example: X Corporation is worth $1 million, exclusive of insurance. A and B each own 50% of X Corp.'s stock, for a stock value of $500,000 each. If the corporation purchases $500,000 of insurance on each of A's and B's lives to fund a stock redemption agreement, at a stockholder's death, the corporation will be worth $1.5 million. If the proceeds are included in the purchase price, A's or B's estate would be entitled to $750,000, and the agreement would be underfunded by $250,000. It would take $1 million of coverage on each of A and B to fully fund this agreement, in a corporation that is worth only $1 million.

On the other hand, it could be argued that the deceased stockholder's estate is being underpaid for the full value of his or her interest in the corporation by not including that excess. This is particularly an issue for family-held corporations under Section 2703, discussed in Chapter Six; as discussed there, the issue under Section 2703 is whether or not parties acting at arm's length would insist on including the insurance proceeds in the purchase price.

The only reported case on this issue is *Blount v. Commissioner*, 428 F.3d 1338 (11th Cir. 2005). In *Blount*, the Eleventh Circuit Court of Appeals held that the value of company stock subject to a corporate redemption agreement should be determined without including the value of the life insurance policies received by the company to fund the buyout. The *Blount* decision reversed a ruling of the Tax Court that the life insurance policies should be included in calculating the corporation's value. The court acknowledged that under the Section 2031 Regulations, in valuing corporate stock, "consideration should also be given to nonoperating assets, including proceeds of life insurance policies to or for the benefit of the company, to the extent that such nonoperating assets have not been taken into account in the determination of net worth." Reg. § 20.2031-2 (f)(2). The Circuit Court concluded, however, that the insurance proceeds were acquired for the sole purpose of funding the company's buyout obligation, and so are not the kind of ordinary non-operating assets that should be included in the company's value under the regulations.

Under a cross-purchase agreement, the funding life insurance is not involved in determining purchase price for purchases either during life or at death, because the policies are owned by the stockholders and not by the corporation.

Chapter Four

State Law Considerations

The preparation of a stock purchase agreement normally focuses on accomplishing the intent of the stockholders regarding their respective interests in preserving the closely held ownership of the stock (e.g., by a group a family members or other small group of existing owners) and/or providing a market for their respective stock holdings upon the occurrence of a triggering event; however, state law considerations must also be taken into account. If the stock purchase agreement provides for a stock redemption upon the occurrence of a triggering event, the parties to the agreement will need to consider the applicable state's law concerning "surplus" requirements before a stock redemption may be made. With respect to individual stockholder's rights under state law, if any of the stockholders are (or were at any time during their ownership of such stock) residents of a community property state, the impact of that state's community property laws (and any state law rights in the stock nominally titled in the name of the stockholder or his or her spouse) should be considered and planned for.

A. Surplus Requirements

Most states require that a purchase by a corporation of its stock (a redemption) must be made out of "surplus." The purpose of such state corporate laws is to protect creditors and other stockholders of the corporation, preventing a redemption that would unduly burden the corporation's ability to meet its liabilities or jeopardize the stock holdings of the other stockholders. Although the term "surplus" is not uniformly defined, the following is a summary of various states' laws with respect to their surplus requirements.

1. Alabama, Arizona, Colorado, Connecticut, Florida, Georgia, Hawaii, Idaho, Indiana, Iowa, Kentucky, Maine, Michigan, Mississippi, Montana, Nebraska, Nevada, New Hampshire, New Mexico, North Carolina, Oregon, Pennsylvania, South Carolina, South Dakota, Tennessee, Utah, Vermont, Virginia, Washington, West Virginia, Wisconsin, and Wyoming all provide that a corporation may not make a distribution in redemption of its stock if it would, as a result, be unable to pay its debts "as they become due in the usual course" of business, or if the corporation's assets would be less than the sum of its liabilities plus the amount that would be needed to satisfy the preferential rights upon dissolution of shareholders whose rights are superior to those receiving the distribution (unless the articles of incorporation permit otherwise).
Ala. Code § 10-2B-6.40; Ariz. Rev. Stat. Ann. § 10-640; Colo. Rev. Stat. § 7-106-401; Conn. Gen. Stat. § 33-687; Fla. Stat. ch. 607.06401; Ga. Code Ann. § 14-2-640; Haw. Rev.

STAT. § 414-111; IDAHO CODE § 30-1-640; IND. CODE ANN. § 23-1-28-3; IOWA CODE § 490.640; KY. REV. STAT. ANN. § 271B.6-400; ME. REV. STAT. ANN. tit. 13-C, § 651; MICH. COMP. LAWS § 450.1345; MISS. CODE ANN. § 79-4-6.40; MONT. CODE ANN. § 35-1-712; NEB. REV. STAT. § 21-2050; NEV. REV. STAT. § 78.288; N.H. REV. STAT. § 293-A:6.40; N.M. STAT. ANN. § 53-11-44; N.C. GEN. STAT. § 55-6-40; OR. REV. STAT. § 60.181; PA. CONS. STAT. § 1551; S.C. CODE ANN. § 33-6-400; S.D. CODIFIED LAWS ANN. § 47-1A-640.1; TENN. CODE ANN. § 48-16-401; UTAH CODE ANN. § 16-10a-640; VT. STAT. ANN. tit. 11A, § 6.40; VA. CODE § 13.1-653; WASH. REV. CODE § 23B.06.400; W. VA. CODE § 31D-6-631; WIS. STAT. § 180.0640; WYO. STAT. § 17-16-640. Virginia, however, provides that a "distribution" does not include the acquisition by a corporation of its shares from the estate or personal representative of a deceased share-holder to the extent it is funded through life insurance proceeds and the board of directors approved the redemption prior to the shareholder's death. VA. CODE § 13.1-603.

2. Alaska's statute provides that a corporation may make a distribution out of retained earnings or in accordance with certain balance sheet and liquidity tests. ALASKA STAT. § 10.06.358. However, a corporation may not make a distribution if it would be "likely to be unable to meet its liabilities as they mature." ALASKA STAT. § 10.06.360. These provisions do not apply to a purchase of shares of a deceased shareholder from life insurance proceeds in excess of the premiums paid by the corporation. ALASKA STAT. § 10.06.368.

3. Arkansas' statute declares that a corporation may not purchase its own shares (A) if there is "a reasonable ground for believing" that the corporation would not be able to meet its obli-gations "as they become due in the usual course of business," or that the value of the remain-ing assets would be less than one and one-fourth times the amount of its liabilities to creditors; or (B) if the net assets remaining would be less than the amount payable to preferred share-holders in the event of liquidation; or (C) if "in respect to purchases out of earned surplus, there are unpaid accrued preferential dividends on shares entitled to priority in respect to dividends over the shares to be purchased." ARK. CODE ANN. § 4-26-611. A corporation may redeem its own shares out of stated capital under certain conditions. *Id.*

4. California permits a corporation to purchase its own assets out of retained earnings, or, if certain balance sheet and liquidity tests are met, absent retained earnings, CAL. CORP. CODE § 500, but the purchase must not impair the ability of the corporation to meet its liabilities as they mature, CAL. CORP. CODE § 501. However, these provisions do not apply to purchases of shares at death under insured stock redemption agreements to the extent proceeds exceed aggregate premiums paid by the corporation for the policy on the life of the deceased stock-holder. CAL. CORP. CODE § 503.1.

5. Delaware prohibits purchases of shares that would impair capital—that is, earned and paid-in surplus can be used. DEL. CODE ANN. tit. 8, § 160. "Surplus" is defined as the excess of net assets over stated capital. DEL. CODE ANN. tit. 8, § 154.

6. District of Columbia law provides that a corporation shall not purchase its own shares "when its net assets are less than the sum of its stated capital, its paid-in surplus, any surplus arising from unrealized appreciation in value or revaluation of its assets and any surplus arising from surrender to the corporation of any of its shares, or when by so doing its net assets would be reduced below such sum." D.C. CODE ANN. § 29-101.05.

7. Illinois allows a corporate distribution in redemption unless, after giving it effect, the corporation would be insolvent or its net assets would be less than zero or less than the maximum payable to shareholders with preferred rights upon dissolution. ILL. REV. STAT. ch. 805, § 5/9.10.

8. Kansas' capital requirement statute prohibits reductions of capital (because of a stock redemption or otherwise) unless the remaining assets would be sufficient to pay any debts for which payment has not been otherwise provided. KAN. CORP. CODE ANN. § 17-6604.

9. Louisiana law provides that a corporation may purchase its own shares out of surplus or, under certain circumstances, out of stated capital. However, it may not purchase its shares when such purchase would render it insolvent or reduce its net assets below the amount payable on liquidation upon shares that have certain preferential rights. LA. REV. STAT. § 12:55. "Surplus" is defined as "the excess of assets over liabilities plus stated capital." LA. REV. STAT. § 12:1.

10. Maryland's statute is the same as those discussed in paragraph 1 above (other than Virginia's life insurance exception), except that "indebtedness" is used instead of "debts." MD. CODE ANN., CORPS. & ASS'NS § 2-311.

11. Massachusetts does not allow a reduction of capital stock if it would render the corporation "bankrupt or insolvent." MASS. GEN. L. ch. 156, § 45. However, the Supreme Judicial Court of Massachusetts has held that the purchase of shares by a corporation does "not necessarily" constitute a reduction of capital stock, since the shares could be resold. *Barrett v. W.A. Webster Lumber Co.*, 175 N.E. 765, 768 (1931).

12. Minnesota allows a corporation to make a distribution in redemption if the board of directors determines that the corporation "will be able to pay its debts in the ordinary course of business after making the distribution." MINN. STAT. § 302A.551.

13. Missouri prohibits a corporation from purchasing its shares if its net assets would be less than its stated capital after the distribution. MO. REV. STAT. § 351.390.

14. New Jersey and North Dakota allow a corporation to make a distribution in redemption, unless the corporation would be unable to pay its debts as they become due in the usual course of its business or the corporation's total assets would be less than its total liabilities. N.J. REV. STAT. § 14A:7-14.1; N.D. CENT. CODE § 10-19.1-92.

15. New York law allows purchases out of "surplus," except where the corporation is or would be rendered insolvent by the purchase. N.Y. BUS. CORP. LAW, § 513. Surplus is defined as "the excess of net assets over stated capital," N.Y. BUS. CORP. LAW § 102(a)(13).

16. Ohio does not allow a corporation to purchase its own shares if doing so would reduce its assets to less than its liabilities plus its stated capital, if any, or if "there is reasonable ground to believe" that it would render the corporation insolvent. OHIO REV. CODE ANN. § 1701.35.

17. Oklahoma law states that no corporation may purchase its own shares if its capital would be impaired, except that it may purchase its preferred shares out of capital under certain circumstances. OKLA. STAT. tit. 18, § 1041.

18. Rhode Island prohibits a redemption or purchase of shares by a corporation unless, after giving it effect, the corporation would be insolvent or its assets would be "less than the sum of its total liabilities plus (unless the articles of incorporation permit otherwise), the amount

that would be needed, if the corporation were to be dissolved at the time of its redemption." R.I. Gen. Laws § 7-1.2-601.

19.   Texas law states that a corporation may not make a distribution in redemption if it would render the corporation insolvent or the distribution would exceed the corporation's surplus. Tex. Corps. & Ass'ns Code § 2.38. "Surplus" is defined as "the excess of the net assets of a corporation over its stated capital." Tex. Corps. & Ass'ns Code § 1.02.

An insured stock redemption agreement will typically mitigate the application of the state's "surplus" requirements. Life insurance death proceeds (more accurately, the excess of policy death proceeds over cash surrender values) create surplus from which the stock of a deceased stockholder may be purchased. Blough, Practical Applications of Accounting Standards 2145 (Ayer Co., February 1981). See also the special provisions of California, Alaska, and Virginia law, above, covering insured stock redemption agreements.

Again, as should be clear, before entering into a stock redemption agreement, the applicable state's law must be reviewed by counsel, to determine what "surplus" requirements, if any, must be met before the corporation may legally redeem its stock, and whether that state law allows creating surplus through asset revaluation.

B. Additional Considerations Where Stock Is Community Property

If any stockholder who is a party to the stockholders' agreement lives in a community property state (or has lived in a community property state during the period of his or her stock holding), then counsel should determine whether the stock subject to the agreement is separate property or community property under that state's law.

If the stock subject to a stockholders' agreement is community property, then the agreement should include additional provisions to address this issue. For example, the non-owner spouse should approve the agreement in writing and consent to the sale by the owner spouse or the owner spouse's estate of the non-owner's one-half community interest in the stock upon the occurrence of a triggering event. The agreement should also contain a provision preventing any attempted testamentary transfer of the one-half community interest in the stock by either spouse to someone other than the other spouse, in the event one predeceases the other. For example, the stockholder-husband could be given a right of first refusal to purchase the wife's community interest in the shares in the case of such an attempted transfer.

Consideration should also be given to what happens if husband and wife divorce or legally separate, as these events dissolve the marital community. For example, the agreement might contain a provision that attempts to prevent the non-owner spouse from becoming a stockholder in his or her own right in case of divorce or separation. This might be accomplished by requiring the owner spouse to purchase the community interest of the non-owner spouse in the shares in such an event.

Chapter Five

Funding and Methods of Payment

Structuring an appropriate method of payments from the corporation and/or the purchasing stockholder(s), as well as how these amounts will be funded, is an important element in planning and drafting an effective stockholders' agreement. Each stockholder who is relying on the stockholders' agreement to create a market for his or her shares of stock will not have confidence in the agreement if it is not adequately funded. Likewise, a stockholders' agreement that is intended to prevent transfers to unwanted third parties may not be effective if adequate funding is not available to purchase the stock upon the occurrence of a triggering event.

A. Lifetime Purchases

For a purchase of shares during the life of a stockholder, the absence of life insurance death proceeds will require a long enough payout period to ensure that the corporation or other stockholders can meet their payment obligations. However, with many policies, high cash values can be created during a stockholder's life, which, after a period of time, can be used to provide all or a substantial part of the purchase price for a *lifetime* buyout. The cash values can be accessed on a tax-favored basis by either policy loan or withdrawal, or by partial surrender of the policy. Loans will be tax-free and withdrawals and surrenders will be tax-free up to the policy owner's basis, unless the policy is a modified endowment contract (as defined in Section 7702A), or unless the "forced-out" gain (FOG) provisions of Section 7702(f)(7) apply.

For the purchase of shares on the total disability of a stockholder, the cash values of the funding life insurance—again, after time—could provide a substantial down payment (as in the case of any other lifetime buyout). The purchase price (in excess of the down payment) should be payable in installments that correspond to the amount of any disability insurance payments received by the purchaser(s). It may also be possible to use a disability policy that is expressly designed for disability buyouts and provides substantial benefits, unrelated to the insured's salary, over a relatively short period of time (perhaps in a lump sum). These types of policies appear to be infrequently used, perhaps because their availability is not generally known or because of their cost (or both).

B. Purchase at a Stockholder's Death

For a purchase at death, life insurance is the funding medium of choice, because it produces the cash needed at the time when it is needed (and does so from the beginning, regardless of when the stockholder's death occurs). Some form of permanent insurance is generally the best choice. Although the premiums for term insurance are initially considerably less expensive than those for permanent insurance, term insurance becomes prohibitively expensive as the stockholders advance in age, and at a certain age (such as 75) it often cannot be renewed. In addition, term insurance creates no cash values to use for a lifetime buyout. Beyond that, the choice of which type of permanent insurance to use will generally be determined by the cash flow requirements of the premium payer(s).

The insurance death proceeds should be designed to provide all—or at least a substantial portion of—the purchase price for the stock of the deceased stockholder (perhaps, as an example, not less than one-third or one-half), and the balance of the purchase price should be payable with adequate interest (at no less than the Applicable Federal Rate) over a relatively short period of time— for example, from three to five or 10 years (although the ability of the purchaser to pay the balance of the purchase price in such a short period of time must be considered). If the stock purchase agreement will not be fully insured, the corporation and/or the stockholders should consider the potential adverse impact. Underinsuring the purchase price often results in placing the deceased stockholder's surviving spouse and family in the position of involuntarily becoming long-term creditors of a business in which they have no voice, and of burdening the surviving stockholders with a substantial obligation to relative strangers who have no interest in the growth of the business.

If the corporation is going to use insurance to fund the purchase of stock held by some, but not all, stockholders at their respective deaths, it should take care to avoid subjecting itself to claims of oppression of the minority stockholders by the "non-insured" minority stockholders. Based on a Delaware case, it appears that if there is a valid business purpose for insuring only some of the stockholders, it will not be found to be oppressive toward the minority stockholders. In *Nixon v. Blackwell*, 626 A.2d 1366 (Del. 1993), the court held that the corporation's practice of using keyman insurance to fund its repurchase obligation to employee stockholders did not treat the non-employee stockholders unfairly. The corporation had a long practice of providing the repurchase benefit to employee stockholders (pursuant to its employee stock ownership plan and otherwise), and there was a legitimate business purpose for doing so.

C. Funding and Payment Issues for Cross-Purchase Agreements

As discussed in Chapter One, paragraph B, under a cross-purchase agreement, the life insurance used to fund the agreement is provided by each stockholder purchasing, owning, and being the beneficiary of a policy in the requisite amount on the life of each of the other stockholders. At the death of any stockholder, the other stockholders will then collect the proceeds of insurance on the deceased stockholder's life—which should collectively allow them to purchase all of the stock from the deceased stockholder's estate. As also noted in Chapter One, the number of policies required so that insurance funding will be provided for regardless of which stockholder dies first can be determined by the formula n(n-1), where n equals the number of stockholders. For example, if three stockholders enter into a stock purchase agreement that provides that at the first death the surviving stockholders will purchase the stock from the deceased stockholder's estate, a total of six life insurance policies will be required; each of the three stockholders will own two policies—one policy insuring the life of each of the other two stockholders.

Again, the number of policies needed can be reduced (to one per shareholder) if a partnership (or an LLC taxed as a partnership) acquires one policy on each stockholder's life for the benefit of the other stockholder/partners. In the above example, the use of a partnership would reduce the number of policies required from six to three. As noted in Chapter One, this alternative is unavailable if the corporation is an S Corporation (because its shares cannot be owned by a partnership or an LLC), although the partnership or LLC could own one policy on each stockholder and pay out the policy death proceeds to the survivors, who would individually carry out the stock purchase. Life insurance funding is simpler under a stock redemption agreement because the corporation purchases, owns, and is the beneficiary of one policy in the requisite amount on the life of each stockholder.

When the cross-purchase format is used, a split-dollar insurance arrangement or a loan arrangement between the corporation and the stockholders could be useful techniques for funding the agreement. In such an arrangement, each stockholder would enter into a split-dollar or loan agreement with the corporation that would provide for the acquisition of a policy in the appropriate amount on the life of each of the other stockholders. This places the principal (or total) burden of paying for the funding insurance on the corporation (where it arguably belongs) and provides sufficient death proceeds to a surviving stockholder to purchase the shares of a deceased stockholder. In addition, the corporation will recover its premium advances or loans at the stockholder's death (which, of course, reduces the death proceeds available to the purchasing stockholders to effect the purchase and, depending on the method used to value the stock of the corporation, may be reflected in the purchase price).

Unlike corporate redemption funding, which involves no income tax cost to the stockholders, in a split-dollar arrangement, each stockholder will report as taxable income each year the "annual economic benefit" of owning insurance policies on the lives of each of his or her co-stockholders with premiums paid by his or her corporation. Traditionally, the economic benefit was measured by the lower of the PS 58 rate (now the Table 2001 rate) or the insurer's one-year published term rates available to all standard risks for each of the co-stockholders. *See* Rev. Ruls. 64-328, 1964-2 C.B. 11 and 66-110, 1966-2 C.B. 12 (now both obsolete), Notice 2002-8 (for pre-final regulation arrangements), and the final split-dollar regulations, Reg. Secs. 1.61-22 and 1.7872-15 (for post-final regulation arrangements). For post-January 28, 2002, arrangements, the alternative term rates must qualify under Rev. Rul. 66-110 and must also be made known to the public and generally sold through the insurer's normal distribution system. *See* Notice 2002-8.

Because the corporation will recover its premium advances at the death of the insured stockholder, it gets no deduction for any part of the premiums advanced. Section 264. The contribution of the economic benefit by the shareholder-owners offsets the otherwise-required inclusion of that amount in their taxable income. However, for post-final regulation arrangements, that contribution is income to the corporation.

The same basic result obtains even if the stockholders are not employees of the corporation. In that situation, any income generated by the arrangement will be treated as a dividend (to the extent of earnings and profits) rather than as compensation. Rev. Rul. 79-50, 1979-1 C.B. 138; *Johnson v. Commissioner*, 71 T.C. 1316 (1968); the split-dollar regulations specifically apply to corporate-shareholder arrangements.

For post-final regulation arrangements, the availability of the "economic benefit regime," measuring the benefit by term costs, depends on policy ownership and whether the corporation is entitled to recover only its premium outlays or the greater of its outlays or the policy's cash value;

other arrangements are taxed under the "loan regime," treating the benefit as the interest that the corporation should have charged on its advances but did not, measured by the Applicable Federal Rate.

For a fuller discussion of post-final regulation split-dollar arrangements, *see* Brody, *Highlights of The Final Split-Dollar Regulations*, J. REPORTS: LAW & POLICY (Jan. 2004), BNA Benefits Practice Center; Brody, Richey & Baier, *Compensating Employees with Life Insurance*, 386 T.M. (2006).

As an alternative, the corporation could lend each stockholder an amount equal to the premiums due on the policies he or she owned on the lives of the other stockholders, and charge interest on those loans at the Applicable Federal Rate, either paid currently or accrued, under a premium-financing agreement.

D. Funding and Payment Issues for the Controlling Stockholder

If one of the stockholders is a controlling stockholder (or could become one, as a result of a purchase under the agreement or otherwise), care must be taken to prevent the corporation from having any incidents of ownership in the policies insuring the life of that stockholder under the split-dollar arrangement, in order to prevent estate taxation of the proceeds in the controlling stockholder's estate. Regulation Section 20.2042-1(c)(6) defines a controlling stockholder as someone who, at the time of his or her death, possesses more than 50% of the total combined voting power of the corporation; however, the 50% requirement is determined without the normal attribution of ownership from the stockholder's family members. If the corporation has any incidents of ownership in a policy on the life of the deceased controlling stockholder that is payable to a third party (e.g., another stockholder for purposes of funding the cross-purchase agreement), the corporation's incidents of ownership will be attributed to the deceased stockholder, causing inclusion of that portion of the policy proceeds in his or her estate for estate tax purposes, regardless of who owned the policy at the insured's death. *See* Rev. Rul. 82-145, 1982-2 C.B. 213, *modifying* Rev. Rul. 76-274, 1976-2 C.B. 278.

Avoiding this potential problem is usually accomplished by prohibiting the corporation from borrowing against, withdrawing from, or exercising any other rights in the policy on the controlling stockholder's life under the pledge of the policy to the corporation under the split-dollar or loan agreement (or by not pledging the policy to the corporation as security for its advances). *See* Ltr. Ruls. 9037012 and especially 9511046, approving a "restricted" collateral assignment arrangement to avoid creating corporate incidents of ownership in the insurance on the controlling stockholder's life. But note that *Estate of Tompkins v. Commissioner, supra,* a case involving interests in a partnership rather than shares of stock in a corporation, and *Estate of Mitchell v. Commissioner, supra,* suggest that both the value of the stock and the insurance proceeds used to fund the stock purchase may not be included in the deceased stockholder's estate in any event. For controlling shareholders, however, the better practice may be to avoid the issue by using the "restricted" collateral assignment arrangement.

See also Finnegan, *Using First-to-Die Life Insurance in Estate Planning*, 21 ESTATE PLANNING 296 (Sept./Oct. 1994), for a thoughtful discussion of the "double inclusion" issue and of using joint, first-to-die insurance to fund a buy-sell agreement.

E. Disposition of Life Insurance Policies Used to Fund a Stockholders' Agreement

The disposition of the funding insurance on the lives of the remaining stockholders following the purchase of the shares of a particular stockholder or the termination of the agreement should be planned for. One method of planning for the disposition of the funding insurance is to provide that on termination of the agreement, each insured stockholder would have the right to acquire the policy(ies) on his or her life from the owner(s), for their "fair market value"—presumably their interpolated terminal reserve value. If a stockholder purchases the policy on his or her life, there will be no transfer-for-value issue, as the insured is an exempt transferee. Similarly, in the event of a lifetime withdrawal from the corporation, the affected stockholder should be given a right to acquire the policy(ies) on his or her life from the owner(s), again for fair market value. Note Rev. Proc. 2005-25, 2005-1 C.B. 992, which defines the fair market value of a policy for purposes of Section 83—applicable to transfers of property in a service environment—as its cash value, excluding surrender and other similar charges.

Following the purchase of shares of a stockholder under a continuing cross-purchase arrangement, the policies owned by the selling stockholder on the lives of his or her co-stockholders will have to be realigned among the stockholders on a cross-owned basis to continue full funding; under a continuing redemption arrangement, there is no similar issue. Again, note the transfer-for-value issue in any such cross-ownership policy transfers (and the use of a partnership or an LLC among the stockholders, possibly unrelated to the insurance, as a potential solution). See Chapter One.

Under a stock redemption agreement, a similar purchase right should be given to each stockholder in the event of termination of the agreement. However, no such purchase right should be given to the remaining (or surviving) stockholders following the purchase of the stock of a particular stockholder, because the corporation will still require the insurance on their lives to purchase their stock. The mere right of a stockholder to purchase a policy on his life under the foregoing circumstances should not give rise to an incident of ownership in the insured stockholder for estate tax purposes. *See Estate of John Smith v. Commissioner*, 73 T.C. 307 (1979), *acq. in result*, 1981-2 C.B. 2; Ltr. Rul. 8049002; *contra* Rev. Rul. 79-46, 1979-1 C.B. 303. However, in Ltr. Rul. 9349002, based on convoluted facts, the insured stockholder was found to have an incident of ownership in a policy held in trust to fund a redemption, because, among other things, upon the termination of the trust, the stockholder had the right to purchase the policy.

This chapter indicates that planning for the appropriate level of funding and the method of payments under a stockholders' agreement is necessary if the agreement is to be effective at the time of a triggering event. To illustrate the cash flow requirements of the arrangement on the parties, it might be helpful to construct a "Stock Purchase Agreement Funding Schedule" when the parties are initially planning the stockholders' agreement. A sample of such a schedule is shown on the following page.

XYZ COMPANY, INC.

Stock Purchase Agreement Funding Schedule
Death Purchase[1]

Stockholder	No. of Shares Owned	Value (at $25 per Share)	Purchaser	No. of Shares Purchased	Purchase Price	Lifetime Purchase[2]	Life Insurance Payable to Purchaser	Funding Deficiency (Excess)
Sam T. Jones	122,000	$3,050,000	RCJ	102,000	$2,550,000	$255,000 down; $29,072/mo.	$300,000	$2,250,000
			LRS	20,000	$ 500,000	$50,000 down; $5,700/mo	$100,000	$ 400,000
				122,000	$3,050,000		$400,000	$2,650,000
Larry R. Smith (LRS) (unrelated key employee)	50,000	$1,250,000	Corp.	50,000	$1,250,000	$125,000 down; $14,251/mo.	$100,000 down;	$1,150,000
Robert C. Jones (RCJ) (son of STJ)	16,000	$ 400,000	Corp.	16,000	$ 400,000	$40,000 down; $4,560/mo.	-0-	$ 400,000
Fred B. Jones (FBJ) (son of STJ)	12,000	$ 300,000	Corp.	12,000	$ 300,000	$30,000 down; $3,420/mo.	-0-	$ 300,000
	200,000	$5,000,000					$500,000	$4,500,000

1. Death Purchase: Entire price payable in cash.
2. Lifetime Purchase: 10% down; balance in equal monthly installments over 10 years, including interest not to exceed 9% (see I.R.C. §1274A).

Chapter Six

Effect of a Stock Purchase Agreement on Valuation for Death Tax Purposes

As previously noted, one of the major purposes of a properly drawn stock purchase agreement has traditionally been to fix the value of the stock of a deceased stockholder at the purchase price provided under the agreement for federal and state estate and inheritance tax purposes. Rev. Rul. 59-60, 1959-1 C.B. 237, *as modified by* Rev. Ruls. 65-192, 1965-2 C.B. 257, 65-193, 1965-2 C.B. 370 and 77-287, 1977-2 C.B. 319. These rulings list the multitude of factors the Internal Revenue Service will consider in valuing a closely held business. The factors considered in these rulings included (but were not limited to):

(a) the nature of the business,
(b) the economic outlook generally and for the specific industry,
(c) the book value of the stock and financial condition of the business,
(d) the company's earning capacity,
(e) the company's dividend-paying capacity,
(f) intangible value, such as goodwill,
(g) prior sales of the stock and the amount of stock to be valued, and
(h) the market price of publicly traded companies in a similar business.

These rulings are so general that today they are not considered useful as guides to valuation in a given situation.

Without a predetermined value for the shares that is binding for estate tax purposes, the estate will have the burden of proving its claimed valuation for the shares. This may lead to increased taxes on what is, in essence, a paper value (if there is no mechanism in place to sell the deceased stockholder's stock at the estate tax valuation), and may result in the expense of contesting this issue with the IRS. Again, if the agreed value does not fix the estate tax value of the stock, in a worst-case scenario, the estate could find that it owes more in estate taxes on the stock than it received for the sale of the stock. As noted in the Introduction and discussed in detail in this chapter, the issue of who will bear the burden of any such additional tax—the purchaser(s) or the decedent's estate—must also be considered. In addition, the valuation understatement penalty imposed by Section 6662(g) may apply; that section imposes a penalty equal to 20% or 40% of any estate or gift tax underpayment (depending on the extent of the undervaluation) attributable to the undervaluation of property if the value claimed is one-half or less of the correct value of the property.

On the other hand, after the enactment of the unlimited estate tax marital deduction in ERTA in 1981, the use of a stock purchase agreement to fix estate tax valuation has become less important, assuming the stockholder is married, the spouse survives, and their estate plan uses the unlimited marital deduction. In those cases, there will be no federal estate tax due at the stockholder's death, regardless of the value of the shares (although state death taxes must be considered, and special planning and drafting is required to obtain the marital deduction when the survivor is a non-U.S. citizen).

Indeed, in some cases, the stockholder's estate may be arguing for as high a value as possible in order to increase the estate's income tax basis for the stock (with no immediate estate tax cost), and the IRS may be contending for a low valuation. However, if the estate overstates the basis using an inflated stock value, the overvaluation penalty of Section 6662 may apply; that section imposes a penalty equal to 20% or 40% of any income tax underpayment (depending on the extent of the overvaluation) attributable to the overvaluation of property if the value claimed on the income tax return is 200% or more of the correct value of the property. *See* Rev. Rul. 85-75, 1985-1 C.B. 376, holding that the fact that a beneficiary's basis for property claimed on her income tax return was the same amount as the value of the property shown on the decedent's estate tax return did not, in itself, show that the beneficiary had reasonable grounds for claiming the basis of that amount for purposes of the overvaluation penalty. Finally, the basis also will be important if the same stock is gifted, sold, or bequeathed in a subsequent transaction by the recipient surviving spouse or the marital trust (especially if it takes place close in time to the stockholder's death).

A. Regulatory and Case Law Development of the Current Estate Tax Valuation Principles

Prior to the adoption of Section 2036(c) (which was retroactively repealed and replaced with Chapter 14 in 1990), it was generally understood that a stock purchase agreement would fix the value of a deceased stockholder's stock for estate tax purposes at the price stated in the agreement if, but *only* if: (1) the agreements were the result of arm's-length negotiations between the parties and, as required by Reg. Sec. 20.2031-2(h), was therefore a "bona fide business arrangement and not a device to pass the . . . shares . . . for less than an adequate and full consideration . . ." to the natural objects of the decedent's bounty (the so-called "device" test); (2) the stockholder was restricted during life from disposing of the stock for more than the price stated in the agreement, e.g., by the grant of a right of first refusal; and (3) at the death of a stockholder, the estate had to sell the stock at the price stated in the agreement to the corporation or the other stockholders, either pursuant to the purchaser's option (not the estate's option) or a mandatory purchase requirement. *See Seltzer v. Commissioner*, TCM 1985-519, and *Weil v. Commissioner*, 22 T.C. 1267 (1954).

If an agreement met the foregoing requirements, the purchase price established by the agreement would constitute a reasonable value for the stock to be purchased at the death of the stockholder, even though in fact the stock might have demonstrably been worth more at the death of the stockholder than the price determined under the agreement. *See generally May v. McGowan*, 194 F.2d 396 (2d Cir. 1952); *Lomb v. Sugden*, 82 F.2d 166 (2d Cir. 1936); *Wilson v. Bowers*, 57 F.2d 682 (2d Cir. 1932); *Commissioner v. Bensel*, 100 F.2d 639 (3d Cir. 1938); *Estate of Littick*, 31 T.C. 181 (1958); and Regulation Section 20.2031-2(h). *See also* TAM 8710004, indicating that when the parties are related, the transaction would be carefully scrutinized to see if it were a "testamentary device."

In *Seltzer*, above, the decedent's stock was subject to a stockholders' agreement which required (in addition to certain lifetime restrictions on the stock) that upon the death of a stockholder, his or her estate was required to offer the stock at book value (as defined in the agreement) to the corporation or, if the corporation did not purchase the stock, to the other stockholders. At the decedent's death, the IRS argued that the stockholders' agreement (providing for a value on the decedent's stock of $251,800) should be ignored for valuation purposes because it did not represent a bona fide business arrangement and because the value established by the agreement (book value) did not include any adjustment for the corporation's goodwill. The Service argued that the proper estate tax value of the stock was $460,000. The Tax Court found the stockholders' agreement effective for purposes of setting the value of the stock at $251,800 for estate tax purposes—the agreement was a bona fide business arrangement because it served to maintain ownership and control for the stockholders. In addition, the court found that if the stockholders chose to not charge each other for the corporation's goodwill, the value for estate tax purposes should not include an adjustment for it. *See also Estate of Bischoff v. Commissioner*, 69 T.C 39 (1977), in which the Tax Court also found that a stockholders' agreement designed to maintain ownership and control within a specific group of stockholders was "grounded on legitimate business considerations."

This point was pushed as far as possible in the case of *Roth v. United States*, 511 F. Supp. 653 (E.D. Mo. 1981), in which the district court upheld a *zero* valuation, arrived at pursuant to a formula stock purchase agreement (based on a multiple of prior years' earnings, and, with the exception of one year, the corporation had lost money in each of the previous seven years). Unfortunately for the taxpayer, the decision was reversed and remanded to the district court for a factual determination of the bona fides of the arrangement, as *St. Louis County Bank v. United States*, 674 F.2d 1207 (8th Cir. 1982). After remand, the case was settled—at a value exceeding zero—with no further reported opinion. In the Eighth Circuit's opinion in *St. Louis County Bank*, the court rejected the lower court's holding that maintaining family control, which provided a business purpose to the arrangement, prevented it from being a "device" to pass the shares for less than full and adequate consideration. The Senate Explanation of new Section 2703, discussed below, approved the Eighth Circuit's approach to this issue.

In *Estate of Joseph H. Lauder v. Commissioner*, TCM 1990-530, the court rejected the taxpayer's summary judgment motion on whether the buy-sell arrangement under review was such a "device" on the grounds that it was a question of fact to be determined at trial on a case-by-case basis. In the trial, reported at TCM 1992-736, the Tax Court held the arrangement (based on a book value theory, with which the estate's own expert disagreed) was a "device" and disregarded it. Finally, in *Lauder III (Estate of Joseph H. Lauder v. Commissioner*, TCM 1994-527), following a trial to determine the fair market value of the stock, the Tax Court provided an in-depth analysis of its determination after ignoring the price used in the stockholders' agreement (based on its findings in the previous two proceedings). Interestingly, the Tax Court also allowed the estate a marital deduction because the low purchase price of the shares increased the value of the remaining shares held by the decedent's spouse. On the other hand, note *Estate of Rudolph v. United States,* 71 A.F.T.R.2d (P-H) 2169 (S.D. Ind. 1993), in which the court upheld an agreed price arrangement between two brothers because the IRS did not establish that, when entered into, the agreement was testamentary in nature.

Section 2036(c), when it was in existence, eliminated the ability of a stock purchase agreement to fix the estate tax valuation of stock owned by a decedent in a family business. As noted above,

Section 2036(c) was effective for transfers after December 17, 1987; it was repealed retroactively by uncodified Section 11601 of OBRA 90, effective October 8, 1990. In the context of a family business stock purchase agreement, if Section 2036(c) applied, it would have caused the stock subject to the agreement to be includible in the deceased stockholder's estate at its date of death fair market value (without regard to the existence of the agreement), preventing the agreement's value from "fixing" the stock's value for estate tax purposes. In addition, while the transfer was to the other stockholders, the deceased stockholder's residuary beneficiary(ies) would normally have had the primary obligation to pay the tax (under a typical tax clause in the decedent's will).

B. Valuation Considerations under Current Law

Section 2703, "Certain Rights and Restrictions Disregarded," enacted as a part of new Chapter 14, provides that for transfer tax purposes—with one important exception, discussed below—the value of property will be determined without regard to an option or other agreement to acquire property (specifically including, under Reg. Sec. 25.2703-1(a)(3), a buy-sell agreement with respect to corporate stock) at less than fair market value.

The Senate Explanation of Section 2703 describes the "estate freeze" aspects of such options as follows:

> Under another common freeze device, a member of an older generation grants a member of a younger generation an option to purchase property at a fixed or formula price. Such an option may be part of a buy-sell agreement under which the survivor (or the corporation) has the right to purchase stock from the estate of the first to die. An option may freeze the value of the property at the strike price which in turn may be below the fair market value of the property at the date of death.

Interestingly, this provision, unlike the rest of Chapter 14, is not limited to family businesses. However, the exception discussed below should mean that practice, in some instances, it may not be a problem among unrelated shareholders. In fact, Reg. Sec. 25.2703-1(b)(3) provides a safe harbor for agreements when more than 50% of the value of the interests is owned directly or indirectly by individuals who are not members of the decedent's family. (For this purpose, family includes anyone described in Reg. Sec. 25.2701-2(b)(5) as well as anyone who is a natural object of the decedent's bounty.) Note the unusual result of this provision in a corporation owned 50/25/25 by three unrelated individuals: qualification for this safe harbor depends on whether it is the 50% stockholder or one of the 25% stockholders who dies first; similarly, in a corporation owned 50/50 by two unrelated individuals, the safe harbor apparently is not available.

The one exception to the rule of Section 2703 is for an option or agreement that is a bona fide business arrangement; that is not a "device to transfer such property to members of the decedent's family"—"natural objects of the decedent's bounty," under Reg. Sec. 25.2703-1(b)(1)—for less than full consideration; and that has terms comparable to those in similar arrangements, entered into in arms'-length transactions. Section 2703(b). The Senate Explanation of Section 2703 gives the following summary of the reasons for the change:

The committee believes that buy-sell agreements are common business planning arrangements and that buy-sell agreements generally are entered into for legitimate business reasons that are not related to transfer tax consequences. Buy-sell agreements are commonly used to control the transfer of ownership in a closely held business, to avoid expensive appraisals in determining purchase price, to prevent the transfer to an unrelated party, to provide a market for the transfer to an unrelated party, to provide a market for the equity interest, and to allow owners to plan for future liquidity needs in advance. However, the committee is aware of the potential of buy-sell agreements for distorting transfer tax value. Therefore, the committee establishes rules that attempt to distinguish between agreements designed to avoid estate taxes and those with legitimate business agreements. These rules generally disregard a buy-sell agreement that would not have been entered into by unrelated parties acting at arm's length.

The same explanation analyzes the provisions as follows:

The bill provides that the value of property for transfer tax purposes is determined without regard to any option, agreement or other right to acquire or use the property at less than fair market value or any restriction on the right to sell or use such property, unless the option, agreement, right or restriction meets three requirements. These requirements apply to any restriction, however created. For example, they apply to restrictions implicit in the capital structure of the partnership or contained in a partnership agreement, articles of incorporation, or corporate bylaws or a shareholders' agreement.

The first two requirements are that the option, agreement, right or restriction (1) be a bona fide business arrangement, and (2) not be a device to transfer such property to members of the decedent's family for less than full and adequate consideration in money or money's worth. These requirements are similar to those contained in the present Treasury regulations, except that the bill clarifies that the business arrangement and device requirements are independent tests. The mere showing that the agreement is a bona fide business arrangement would not give the agreement estate tax effect if other facts indicate that the agreement is a device to transfer property to members of the decedent's family for less than full and adequate consideration. In making this clarification, it adopts the reasoning of *St. Louis County Bank* [*supra*] and rejects the suggestion of other cases that the maintenance of family control standing alone assures the absence of a device to transfer wealth.

In addition, the bill adds a third requirement, not found in present law, that the terms of the option, agreement, right or restriction be comparable to similar arrangements entered into by persons in an arm's-length transaction. This requires that the taxpayer show that the agreement was one that could have been obtained in an arm's-length bargain. Such determination would entail consideration of such factors as the expected term of the agreement, the present value of the property, its expected value at the time of exercise, and [the] consideration offered for the option. It is not met simply by showing isolated comparables but requires a demonstration of the general practice of unrelated parties. Expert testimony would be evidence of such practice. In unusual cases where comparables are difficult to find because the taxpayer owns a unique business, the taxpayer can use comparables from similar businesses.

The bill does not otherwise alter the requirements for giving weight to a buy-sell agreement. For example, it leaves intact present law rules requiring that an agreement have lifetime restrictions in order to be binding on death.

Accordingly, Section 2703 is a codification of pre-Section 2036(c) regulatory and case law (as described above), with the addition of an independent arm's-length or comparability test. Section 2703 and Reg. Sec. 25.2703-1(b)(2) make clear that each test is independent and must be separately met to have the agreement respected. This new test may require expert testimony (presumably at the time the agreement is being planned and drafted) to determine whether non-related parties would have entered into a similar arrangement. The Senate Finance Committee Report to Section 2703 suggests this as a possibility; it is unclear, however, who has the expertise to provide an opinion on this issue (or who would be willing to do so, and at what price).

Three recent cases provide some guidance—but little certainty—on this test. *Smith v. United States*, 94 AFTR 2d (W.D. Pa., 2004), *Blount v. Commissioner*, 428 F.3d 1338 (11th Cir. 2005), and *Amlie v. Commissioner*, TCM 2006-76. In *Smith*, the court held that affidavits from attorneys that an installment payment provision in a buyout was "common" was not enough to support summary judgment.

In *Blount*, the court discounted expert testimony which it concluded did not provide evidence of comparability. The taxpayer's professional appraiser testified that the fixed purchase price set by the buy-sell agreement was fair market value. However, the Tax Court concluded (and the Eleventh Circuit agreed) that the expert "failed to provide any evidence of similar arrangements actually entered into by parties acting at arm's length, as required by Section 2703(b)(3)," and that the expert's conclusion that the terms of the buy-sell agreement were comparable to similar arms-length agreements was "unsupportable." *Blount*, TCM 2004-116 at 748.

In *Amlie*, the Tax Court held that a buy-sell agreement between family members was effective in establishing the date of death value of closely held bank stock for estate tax purposes, despite the fact that the fair market value was much higher. The court concluded that the taxpayer had satisfied each of the Section 2703 requirements for the agreement to be respected, including the difficult comparability test. In satisfying the comparability test, the estate was able to show that the terms of the buy-sell agreement were originally part of an earlier negotiated and arm's-length agreement with an unrelated banking group. In addition, the fixed purchase price was determined by a valuation expert and based upon comparable sales and merger transactions involving banks in the region. The *Amlie* case illustrates that although the Section 2703 comparability test is a difficult one, it can be satisfied under the right set of facts.

Under Reg. Sec. 25.2703-1(b)(4), an agreement will meet the comparability test if it is one that could have been "obtained in a fair bargain among unrelated parties in the same business, dealing . . . at arm's length"; a fair bargain is one that conforms with the general practice of unrelated parties under negotiated agreements, taking into account the expected term of the agreement, the current fair market value of the stock, anticipated changes in value during the term, and any consideration paid. With the exception of "great facts" cases as in *Amlie*, it is unlikely that many family arrangements in which the purchase price will be below fair market value would be able to meet this formulation of the new test, especially given the Regulation's apparent emphasis on the effect of the term of the arrangement and anticipated changes in value during the term on a fixed-price agreement.

This codification of the prior regulatory tests was thought to signal a renewed interest in this area by the IRS—a conclusion supported by the attention given to it in the *Smith, Blount,* and *Amlie* cases—and would appear to present a formidable hurdle to such a use of stock purchase agreements in family businesses. Nevertheless, stock purchase agreements will continue to be used in family business settings for their non-tax benefits (such as keeping the shares in the hands of the desired control group). Again, non-family businesses presumably would be able to meet this new third test, and many would qualify for the regulatory more than 50% nonfamily-ownership safe harbor, discussed above.

Section 2703 is effective for agreements entered into or "substantially modified" after October 8, 1990. It is unclear from the statute what will be considered a "substantial modification" of a pre-10/9/90 agreement—can a new stockholder be added (or deleted), can the agreed price be changed (up or down), can the payment terms be changed, etc.? *See* Ltr. Rul. 9141043, which approved what appears to be such an insignificant change—the par value of the shares—that one wonders why it was even an issue.

Under Reg. Sec. 25.2703-1(c)(1), any discretionary modification of an agreement (whether or not authorized by its terms) that results in other than a de minimis change to the "quality, value, or timing of the rights of any party" is a substantial modification. Furthermore, that Regulation Section provides that if the terms require periodic updating, the failure to update (probably based on a suspicion that the value had increased) is presumed to substantially modify the agreement. Finally, it holds that the addition of a family member to the agreement is considered a substantial modification, unless the addition is mandatory under the agreement or the added family member is in a generation no lower than that of the youngest person who is a party to the agreement (e.g., in an agreement between two brothers, the addition of a third brother will not be a substantial modification, but the addition of a nephew will—unless the addition is mandatory under the agreement).

On the other hand, under subsection (2) of that Regulation Section, (i) a modification required by the agreement; (ii) a discretionary modification that doesn't change the rights or restrictions under the agreement (*see* Ltr. Rul. 9432017); (iii) a modification of a capitalization rate tied to an outside index (*see* Ltr. Rul. 9322035); or (iv) a modification that results in a better approximation of fair market value (*see* Ltr. Rul. 9417007) are not considered substantial modifications. *See also* Ltr. Rul. 9152031, which approved a change to a grandfathered agreement that provided for reviewing the value every five years rather than annually. *See also Blount v. Commissioner,* above, holding that changes to a grandfathered agreement were "substantial," requiring consideration of comparability under Section 2703.

In Blount, the buy-sell agreement was originally executed in 1981, long before the effective date of Section 2703, and the modification was executed in 1996. Because the buy-sell agreement included a reduced purchase price and the elimination of an installment payment option, the Tax Court concluded (and the Eleventh Circuit agreed) that the modification resulted in more than a de minimis change, and as a result, the agreement became subject to Section 2703.

In Ltr. Rul. 9432017, the IRS provided several examples of changes that may be made to buy-sell agreements without affecting the "grandfathered" status of an agreement for Section 2703 purposes. A change in the agreed-upon redemption price (or the formula for determining the redemption price) will not be a substantial modification if the new price (or formula) more closely reflects the stock's fair market value. Additionally, a change in the interest rate (for redemptions occurring over time) that provides a minimum floor and maximum ceiling on the rate that can be paid and, therefore, provides a certain amount of risk and protection for both the company and the stockholder (assuming the range of interest rates is fairly representative of market rate fluctuations) was found to be de minimis. The IRS also appeared to have viewed all of the changes proposed in Ltr. Rul. 9432017 together to determine if there was a substantial modification to the agreement. A reduction in certain circumstances of the redemption down payment required by the corporation may have otherwise been considered a substantial modification; however, when the reduction occurred only because of a higher purchase price provided by another change to the agreement at the same time, the IRS found that the reduced down payment only modified the favorable treatment to the redeemed stockholder from the other change—and, viewing these modifications together, still resulted in a price that more closely approximated fair market value.

Regulation Sec. 25.2703 was effective as of January 28, 1992; for modifications to stockholders' agreements before that date, taxpayers can rely on "any reasonable interpretation" of the statute to determine if a substantial modification has taken place.

For a "grandfathered" agreement—which, under prior law, actually would have worked to fix estate tax values at the purchase price provided under the agreement (and many of which, to the surprise of practitioners and their clients, probably would have failed), any changes should be viewed as potential substantial modifications and approached cautiously. If the grandfathered agreement does not work to fix estate tax values even under prior law, changes can be made without this concern.

Obviously, the inability in a family business to fix estate tax values through the use of a stock purchase agreement may make such an agreement less desirable, but, as noted above, most closely held businesses will want to use them to restrict the transferability of their shares. If Section 2703 prevents the use of a fixed purchase price in the agreement, insurance funding may be more difficult because of the "moving target" of value. Perhaps family business buy-sell agreements will be intentionally overfunded at the outset, or some sort of guaranteed insurability feature will be incorporated into the insurance funding (allowing additional coverage to be obtained in the future, without evidence of insurability). In any event, deferred payment of any unfunded portion of the purchase price by the purchaser(s) will likely continue to be important, to allow them to pay off any unfunded balance of the purchase price over time.

It is possible that for stock purchase agreements subject to Section 2703, the entire concept of trying to use an agreement to fix values for estate tax purposes in family businesses will have to be reconsidered. If values cannot be fixed for estate tax purposes, perhaps not requiring a sale at death under the agreement—but allowing the shares to be left only to the "active" children or a surviving spouse (or anyone in the "control group")—would make sense in many cases. Obviously, if the shares go to a surviving spouse (or a marital trust), the estate tax issue gets deferred until his or her death (when it will again become critical, if the shares are still owned by the survivor or the trust). An alternative to using an agreement to fix values in a family business—which will provide a "valuation floor" for the IRS—would be to give the other family members a call option to purchase the stock from the decedent's estate or revocable trust. Such a call option should not set a floor for the price, as the deceased stockholder's estate does not have the right to sell at that price.

As another alternative, when continuing to use a stock purchase agreement in a family business for non-tax purposes (especially control) makes sense, given the effects of Section 2703, the agreement could require a purchase at an objectively determined fair market value (perhaps based on an appraisal) without regard to the terms of the agreement. Again, the difficult insurance funding and/ or financing issues involved in such an arrangement must be considered.

As noted in Chapter One, if the agreement attempts to fix the estate tax value of the shares at the price determined in the agreement but fails to do so, not only would the decedent's estate owe an estate tax on the higher value (and the estate tax might be more than the purchase price), but there is the issue of who bears the burden of the additional tax generated by the increased share value. Under a typical tax clause in many stockholders' wills or revocable trusts, *all* transfer taxes (including those generated by the increased share value) are to be paid out of the residuary estate—meaning the decedent's family members who are the residuary beneficiaries will be liable for the estate tax on the increased value, which benefited the purchaser of the shares. If the residuary beneficiary were a spouse or marital trust, the payment of estate taxes from that bequest would disqualify that part of the bequest for the marital deduction, increasing the tax, reducing the deduction, etc. An attempt in the tax clause to place the burden of any such tax directly on the purchaser would, of course, highlight the issue. Perhaps using a general tax clause providing for full apportionment of all transfer taxes would make sense in any estate when a stock purchase agreement attempts to fix estate tax values at the agreed price.

Chapter Seven

Income Tax Characteristics of the Stock Purchase Agreement—Problems Common to Both Cross-Purchase and Stock Redemption Forms of Agreement

The parties to an agreement should consider what impact the agreement will have on how insurance premiums in an insured stock purchase plan will be treated for income tax purposes and how the purchase or sale of the stock will be taxed.

A. Nondeductibility of Insurance Premiums

No income tax deduction is allowed for premiums paid on life insurance used to fund a stockholders' agreement, regardless of the form of the agreement, because the corporation will be a beneficiary, directly or indirectly, of at least part of the death benefit under the policy. Section 264(a)(1).

In choosing between stock redemption and cross-purchase arrangements, a comparison should be made of the relative income brackets of the corporation and the stockholders, so that premiums will be paid at the lowest before-tax cost. If the corporation is in a higher tax bracket than the stockholders, a method of achieving the lowest before-tax cost for premiums is to use a cross-purchase arrangement and have the corporation pay tax-deductible salary increases or bonuses to the stockholders sufficient to pay the life insurance premiums *plus* the tax on the salary increase or bonus. Payment of income tax by the lower-bracket employee-stockholder on the increased compensation will be less than the income tax that would have otherwise been paid by the corporation in the absence of the income tax deduction for the additional employee compensation. However, there is always the danger under a cross-purchase arrangement that salary increases or bonuses used to pay premiums will be disallowed as corporate deductions because they are unreasonable (I.R.C. Section 162), thus resulting in double-taxation of the payments. It is also important to keep in mind that the relative tax brackets of the corporation and the shareholders may change over time.

If a cross-purchase arrangement is used, but a split-dollar or loan arrangement is used to provide the funding insurance, the corporation will pay the major portion (or all) of the premiums. Thus, insofar as the economics of who pays the premiums is concerned, there will be little distinction between stock redemption and cross-purchase arrangements with split-dollar or loan funding. As a result, if the corporation is in a lower tax bracket than the stockholders, the lowest before-tax cost for premiums can be achieved either by using a stock redemption arrangement or by using a cross-purchase arrangement combined with split-dollar or a loan.

B. Taxation of Insurance Premiums

Under a stock redemption arrangement, there are no tax consequences to the stockholders resulting from corporate premium payments, as the payments are not dividends to the stockholders. *Prunier v. Commissioner*, 248 F.2d 818 (1st Cir. 1957); *Sanders v. Fox*, 253 F.2d 855 (10th Cir. 1958); Rev. Rul. 59-184, 1959-1 C.B. 65. Under a cross-purchase arrangement, any life insurance premiums directly paid by the corporation on policies owned by the stockholders will be taxed as a dividend to the stockholder owning the policy, or, arguably, as compensation, if the stockholder were an employee as well. *Cf., Doran v. Commissioner*, 246 F.2d 934 (9th Cir. 1957). However, as noted in Chapter Five, if a split-dollar arrangement is used to fund the premiums, the stockholder will be taxed on the annual economic benefit attributable to the amount at risk under an economic benefit regime arrangement or on the imputed interest under a loan regime arrangement. Chapter Nine discusses this issue in situations in which the corporation is an S Corporation.

C. Taxation of Policy Proceeds

Absent a transfer for value of the policy (or an interest in the policy during the stockholder's life), the receipt of the proceeds of life insurance on the life of a deceased stockholder by the corporation (in a stock redemption arrangement) or the surviving stockholders (in a cross-purchase arrangement) will be income tax-free. Section 101(a)(1). However, as noted in Chapter One, Section 101(j), added by the COLI Best Practices provisions of the Pension Protection Act of 2006, provides an exception to that rule for certain employer-owned policies issued after August 17, 2006, making the proceeds in excess of premiums paid taxable income, unless that Section's notice, consent, and eligibility requirements are met before the policies are issued. As noted in Chapters One and Five, under a cross-purchase arrangement, if the surviving stockholders acquire the policies on each other's lives owned by the deceased stockholder, there will have been a transfer of those policies for a valuable consideration, unless the stockholders are also partners in a partnership (or are otherwise exempt transferees). As a result, part of the death proceeds will be subject to income tax under the transfer-for-value rule of Section 101(a)(2).

As discussed in Chapter One, there is an exception to the transfer-for-value rule for the transfer of a policy to a corporation in which the insured is a stockholder (or an officer), but there is no similar exception for a transfer from a corporation to a stockholder. Thus, a switch can always be made income tax-free from a cross-purchase to a stock redemption arrangement, but not vice versa. Consequently, if there is doubt about which form of agreement to initially use (as in planning a Wait-and-See Buy-Sell Agreement), it is safer to start with a cross-purchase arrangement. Similarly, there is an exception to the transfer-for-value rule for transfers among partners, but *not* for transfers among co-shareholders (unless they are also partners or members of an LLC). As also discussed in Chapter One, one planning technique to avoid this issue is to have the stockholders also be partners in a state law valid partnership or members of a state law valid LLC, whether or not the partnership's (or the LLC's) business is related to that of the corporation. See the discussion in Chapter One, citing Ltr. Ruls. 9042023, 9235029, 9239033, 9309021, and 9410039 and Rev. Proc. 96-12; note also Ltr. Rul. 9625013, reaching the same conclusion for members of an LLC taxed as a partnership. *See also* Brody & Leimberg, *The Not So Tender Trap*, above.

D. Treatment of the Purchase Price by the Buyer

The purchase price paid by the purchaser for the stock of the selling stockholder is not deductible by the purchaser for income tax purposes regardless of the format chosen. As noted in Chapter One, paragraph F, under a cross-purchase arrangement, each purchasing stockholder receives an income tax basis for the shares purchased equal to the cost of the shares. Under a stock redemption arrangement, there is no increase in basis for the remaining or surviving stockholders as a result of the stock purchase by the corporation (although note the discussion, in Chapter Nine, of this issue in an insurance-funded arrangement in an S Corporation setting).

For example, assume that three stockholders each own 100 shares of stock (representing all of the outstanding stock), each with a cost basis and fair market value of $100. If, on the death of the first stockholder, his or her shares are redeemed through a stock redemption agreement, the surviving two stockholders continue to have a cost basis in their stock of $100. However, each surviving stockholder's 100 shares now represents one-half of the outstanding stock—the value of which would have, therefore, increased to $150 (assuming the value of the corporation is not reduced by the redemption—for example, when it is fully insured); the redemption agreement caused a built-in "phantom" gain of $50 for each of the surviving two stockholders' holdings—even though the underlying value of the corporation did not change. On the other hand, had these same three stockholders used a cross-purchase stockholders' agreement, at the first death the surviving stockholders would have each purchased $50 worth of the deceased stockholder's stock, and the purchasing stockholders' bases in these purchased shares would also be $50. After the cross-purchases, each of the two surviving stockholders would have held 150 shares of stock with a cost basis of $150—there would be no built-in "phantom" gain.

As a general rule, under a stock redemption arrangement, the corporate stock purchase will not cause the increased proportionate interests of the remaining or surviving stockholders to be taxed to them as a dividend. *Holsey v. Commissioner*, 258 F.2d 865 (3d Cir. 1958) and Rev. Rul. 58-614, 1958-2 C.B. 920. However, dividend treatment will apply if the remaining or surviving stockholders had a primary and unconditional obligation to purchase the stock, which the corporation satisfies (*Wall v. United States*, 164 F.2d 462 (4th Cir. 1947) and Rev. Rul. 69-608, 1969-2 C.B. 104), or they end up owning the purchased shares (*Zipp v. Commissioner*, 259 F.2d 119 (6th Cir. 1958); *Stephens v. Commissioner*, 60 T.C. 1004 (1973), *aff'd*, 506 F.2d 1400 (6th Cir. 1974)). *Cf.,* Section 305(c) and Regulation Section 1.305-3(e), Ex. (10). Obviously, if the stockholders are obligated under the agreement to buy the shares, the stockholders' agreement must not require or even allow the corporation to use its funds to purchase the shares for the benefit of the other stockholders, nor to discharge their legal obligation to purchase the shares.

E. Taxation of the Purchase Price to the Seller

Under a cross-purchase arrangement, the sale of shares by a stockholder during life will result in capital gain or loss. A sale at death under a cross-purchase agreement will normally result in little, if any, gain or loss because the stock of the deceased stockholder will receive a new, stepped-up (or stepped-down) basis equal to fair market value at death, under Section 1014, except for decedents dying in 2010, and, presumably, fair market value will equal the purchase price (as long as too much time has not passed between the date of death and the date of the sale). Thus, no gain will result from the sale and no income tax will result. If the stock is community property, the same favorable tax consequences apply at the death of either the stockholder spouse or other spouse, since, under Section 1014, both the deceased spouse and the surviving spouse receive a stepped-up basis in their respective one-half community interests in the stock.

On the other hand, as discussed in Chapter Eight, when the corporation has earnings and profits (even if it is an S Corporation, but has prior C Corporation earnings and profits), under a stock redemption arrangement, the same favorable tax results will occur *if and only if* the redemption qualifies as an exchange (a capital transaction) under the rules of Section 302 (with the overlay of the Section 318 attribution rules) or under the special rules of Section 303 (relating to the redemption of stock to pay estate tax). Note the potential effect of the provisions of the 2003 Act on this issue—reducing the maximum rate on qualifying dividends to 15% through 2008.

F. Interest on Deferred Payments

Sections 1274 and 1274A, added to the Code by the Tax Reform Act of 1984 and the Imputed Interest Simplification Act of 1985, respectively, add considerable complexity to avoiding the imputation of interest in connection with deferred payment sales. Subject to specified statutory exceptions, the Sections apply to all seller-financed sales or exchanges of property that is not publicly traded when all or a part of the consideration received is a nonpublicly traded debt instrument. This broad coverage clearly encompasses sales of stock under a stock purchase agreement in which the seller receives the buyer's debt obligation for all or part of the purchase price.

If Section 1274 applies to a deferred payment sale (because inadequate interest is provided), interest will be imputed to the seller as income (and deductible by the buyer, subject to the interest classification rules of Section 163, if the buyer is an individual or a stockholder in an S Corporation redemption) at a prescribed rate, and both seller and buyer will be required to account for their respective interest income and interest expense on the accrual method, using the complicated original issue discount (OID) rules.

The provisions of these Sections can be briefly summarized as follows:

(1)   If the seller-financed debt is $2.8 million (indexed for inflation after 1989) or less, under Section 1274A, the payment of interest at the rate of 9% compounded semi-annually, or if less, at the applicable federal rate compounded semi-annually, will avoid the imputed interest rules. Failure to pay interest at this safe harbor rate will result in the imputation of interest based on the same applicable federal rate.

(2)   If the seller-financed debt exceeds $2.8 million (as similarly indexed for inflation), the payment of interest at the applicable federal rate compounded semi-annually will avoid the imputed interest rules. Failure to pay interest at this safe harbor rate will result in the imputation of interest based on the same rate.

(3)   If the imputed interest rules apply (e.g., interest is not paid at the safe harbor rate), under Section 1274A, the seller and buyer will be able to elect the cash method of accounting for interest income and expense if the seller financing is $2 million (again, as indexed for inflation after 1989) or less and the *seller* (e.g., the selling stockholder or his or her estate) is not an accrual basis taxpayer or a dealer with respect to the property sold or exchanged. In the

absence of qualification for this exception and making the required election, the seller and buyer must both account for interest on the accrual method.

(4) The applicable federal rate (AFR) is published monthly by the IRS. There are three AFRs, depending on the term of the debt:

Short term = demand or term of 3 years or less
Mid-term = term over 3 years but not over 9 years
Long-term = term over 9 years

(5) All interest calculations assume semi-annual compounding. For example, if seller financing is $2.8 million (as indexed for inflation) or less and the parties use the 9% safe harbor rate, then, to avoid the imputed interest rules, either interest must be payable at least semi-annually or an equivalent interest rate must be used that corresponds with the payment period selected. The published AFRs provide annual, semi-annual, quarterly, and monthly interest equivalents for each AFR term. For example, 9% compounded semi-annually equals 9.20% compounded annually; 8.90% compounded quarterly; and 8.84% compounded monthly.

(6) In determining the applicable AFR, the AFR will be the "lowest 3-month rate"—that is, the AFR in the month in which a binding written contract exists for the sale or exchange, or, if lower, the AFR in either of the two preceding months. In the case of a buy-sell agreement, it is unclear if the applicable AFR should be determined when the agreement is signed or when the sale takes place; conservatism suggests using the applicable AFR at the date of sale.

(7) Prior to the Tax Reform Act of 1984, the imputed interest rules for deferred payment sales were contained in Section 483. That Section continues to coexist, in modified form, with Section 1274. In some cases, Section 483 will apply when Section 1274 does not; for example, a sale of property when the total purchase price, including down payment, principal balance, *and* aggregate interest payments, is $250,000 or less. Because the safe harbor rate provided in Section 483 is the same as in Section 1274, paying interest at that rate will avoid the imputed interest rules of Section 483 as well as those of Section 1274.

(8) The imputed interest rules are generally effective for sales or exchanges made after June 30, 1985.

As discussed in Chapter One, paragraph D, the interest on deferred payments made by the individual stockholders under a cross-purchase arrangement, or by an S Corporation under a stock redemption arrangement, will also be subject to the limits on deductibility provided by the interest classification rules of Section 163.

G. Use of the Installment Method of Recognizing Gain

If the selling stockholder is not a dealer in securities, the stock being sold is not traded on an established securities market, and the selling stockholder will receive at least one payment after the close of the taxable year in which the disposition occurs, he or she will recognize the gain from such sale under the installment method provided under Section 453, unless an election is made to opt out of that treatment. The installment method permits the selling stockholder to spread the payment of the tax liability arising from the sale over the period in which payments are received. The gain recognized from a sale for any taxable year is the proportion of the principal payments received in that year that the gross profit (realized or to be realized when payment is to be completed) bears to the total contract price. Interest paid on the deferred principal payments by the purchaser is treated as ordinary income to the selling stockholder and, subject to the interest classification provisions under Section 163, may or may not be fully deductible by the purchaser.

> Example: A, a non-dealer in securities, sells her nonpublicly-traded stock in X Corporation to B for $1 million, payable in 10 annual installments of $100,000 each plus adequate stated interest. A's basis in the stock is $200,000. Her gross profit from the sale is $800,000 (the sales price of $1 million less $200,000 basis). The gross profit ratio is 80% ($800,000 gross profit divided by the $1 million sales price). Accordingly, $80,000 (80% of $100,000) of each $100,000 principal payment is recognized as gain attributable to the sale. The interest received will be ordinary income to A.

A selling stockholder who is permitted to use the installment method under Section 453 may elect not to use the method and, instead, recognize all of the income from the sale in the year of the disposition. The stockholder must make such an election, in the manner prescribed by regulations, on or before the due date (including extensions) for filing the return for the tax year in which the disposition occurs. Once such an election is made, it may be revoked only with the consent of the Secretary of the Treasury.

The receipt of a bond or other evidence of indebtedness by the selling stockholder will not be treated as a payment under the installment method, unless the bond or evidence of indebtedness is payable on demand or is readily tradable. If a stockholder receives an installment obligation as part of a plan of complete corporate liquidation under Section 331, the receipt of such obligation may or may not be considered a payment. The rules pertaining to complete liquidations will not be discussed here, as they are not usually relevant to a stock purchase under a stock redemption agreement.

If the selling stockholder pledges an installment obligation received from the sale of property (other than certain excluded property) having a sales price exceeding $150,000 as security for any indebtedness, the amount of indebtedness so secured will be considered a constructive payment on the obligation and taxed accordingly.

If the installment method is used in a sale to a related person, the amount realized by the related person from a subsequent disposition of the stock within two years from the initial sale and prior to the receipt by the selling stockholder of all of the payments due from the related person will be treated as being constructively received by the selling stockholder and taxed accordingly. For the purpose of imposing constructive receipt on the selling stockholder, a "related person" is a sibling (whether by the whole or half-blood), a spouse, an ancestor, a lineal descendant, and certain partnerships, trusts, and corporations; however, a sale or exchange of stock to the issuing corporation (i.e., a stock redemption) is not treated as a sale to a related person.

Payments received by a related person from a subsequent disposition of the note will not be treated as being constructively received by the selling stockholder if the disposition occurred as the result of an involuntary conversion or a death; if it is established, to the satisfaction of the Secretary of Treasury, that neither the initial sale by the selling stockholder nor the subsequent disposition by the related person had as one of its principal purposes the avoidance of federal income tax; or if the second disposition occurs more than two years after the date the stockholder sold the stock to the related person. The running of the two-year period cutting off constructive receipt to the selling stockholder is tolled during any period in which the related person's risk of loss with respect to such stock is substantially diminished by the holding of a put with respect to such stock, the existence of another person's right to acquire the stock, a short sale, or any other similar transaction.

Section 453A provides that if the aggregate face amount of all installment obligations owned by the seller (as of the close of the tax year in which the sale of the stock occurs) exceeds $5 million, and the installment sales of property (other than certain types of excluded property, such as the personal use property of an individual, property used or produced in the trade or business of farming, and timeshares and residential lots with respect to which interest is paid) in that year had sales prices exceeding $150,000, the seller must pay interest on a portion of the tax deferred under such installment obligations. The interest payable by the seller is on the amount of taxes deferred by such installment obligations attributable to their aggregate face amount outstanding at the close of the year in excess of the $5 million threshold. Although payable as additional tax, any interest paid on the deferred tax liability is subject to the deductibility limitation rules of Section 163 for interest on tax underpayments. For such "large" installment sales, this provision obviously takes much of the tax deferral (that is, the time value of money) benefit out of an installment sale transaction.

Section 453A also provides that if a taxpayer pledges such an obligation to secure a debt, the taxpayer must recognize, as a constructive payment on such obligation for the purposes of Section 453, an amount equal to the amount of the debt so secured. For the purposes of determining whether an installment obligation arises from the disposition of property having a sales price exceeding $150,000 and is thus subject to Section 453A, all sales or exchanges that are a part of the same transaction (or a series of related transactions) are treated as one sale or exchange.

For installment obligations subject to Section 453A, interest must be paid on the tax deferred under the installment method to the extent attributable to the amount by which the face amount of all such obligations held by the seller that arose during, and are outstanding at the close of, such taxable year exceed $5 million. In determining whether the $5 million threshold has been exceeded for any taxable year, the face amount of installment obligations arising during the year and outstanding as of the close of the year is reduced by the amount treated as a payment on such obligations for such taxable year under the pledge rule, discussed above.

The amount of interest payable by the seller under Section 453A is the applicable percentage of the deferred tax liability with respect to such obligations multiplied by the underpayment rate under Section 6621 (the applicable federal short-term rate plus three percentage points) in effect for the month within which the taxable year ends. The deferred tax liability with respect to such installment obligations is the amount of gain under the obligations that has not been recognized as of the close of the taxable year multiplied by the maximum rate of tax in effect for such taxable year. This rate will vary depending on whether the taxpayer is a corporation, an individual, an estate, or a trust. As noted above, the interest paid on the deferred tax liability, although payable as additional tax, is subject to the deductibility rules of Section 163 for interest on tax underpayments.

The applicable percentage for installment obligations arising in a taxable year is computed by dividing the portion of the aggregate face amount of the installment obligations subject to Section 453A outstanding as of the close of the year over $5 million by the aggregate face amount of such installment obligations outstanding as of the close of the taxable year. This percentage will not change as payments are made (or deemed made under the pledge rule) in subsequent taxable years when determining future interest payments on the deferred tax liability arising from the installment obligations received in the year for which the applicable percentage is computed.

The computations under Section 453A can be summarized for planning purposes as follows:

1. For "large" installment sales, the effect of Section 453A is to eliminate much of the tax deferral (the time value of money) benefit from such a sale.

2. Installment sales in a given taxable year must exceed $5,000,000 in order for Section 453A to apply. Therefore, stretching out large installment sales over several years should be considered, so that no individual year's installment sale exceeds $5,000,000. However, this "stretch-out" technique must not cause other tax problems, such as violation of the partial redemption rules of Section 302, discussed in Chapter Eight.

3. For a sale of stock at death by an estate or revocable trust after the owner's death, Section 453A will have little practical impact. Because of the stock's step-up (or step-down) in basis at death, except for decedent's dying in 2010, there will be little, if any, gain deferred, and therefore little, if any, deferred tax liability subject to the interest penalty imposed by the Section.

4. In case of a stock sale by an individual during his or her lifetime, the interest penalty paid under Section 453A will not be deductible, as it will be classified as nondeductible personal interest under Section 163 by Regulation 1.163-9T(b)(2).

Chapter Eight

Income Tax Characteristics Peculiar to the Stock Redemption Agreement

The income tax issues discussed in Chapter Seven relate to both cross-purchase and stock redemption agreements. This chapter focuses on additional important income tax characteristics that are peculiar only to the stock redemption agreement.

A. In General

If, but only if, the redemption qualifies under Sections 302 or 303 as an exchange of stock, the sale of stock by a stockholder to his or her corporation (a redemption) will be treated as received in exchange for the stock so that it will be a capital transaction, resulting in a capital gain or loss after recovery of basis. At the death of a stockholder (assuming the redemption price is the same as the estate tax value for the stock), such a sale to the corporation will be income tax-free, because the stock's basis will be stepped-up to the estate tax value at the death of the deceased stockholder (except for decedents dying in 2010). However, absent a qualifying redemption under Sections 302 or 303, the *entire* payment (not just the portion representing the capital gain) received by the stockholder (or his or her estate) for the stock will be treated as a *dividend, taxable as ordinary income* (to the extent of sufficient corporate earnings and profits). Sections 302(d), 301(c), and 316(a).

In essence, there is no recovery of basis if the payment is a dividend; a "disappearing basis" situation. As noted in Chapter Nine, this will not be an issue for an S Corporation with no accumulated C Corporation earnings and profits. Most important, as noted in Chapter Seven, the lowering of the rate on qualifying dividends (the maximum federal rate is 15% through at least 2010) will, while it is in effect, reduce the importance of this issue.

B. Section 302 Redemptions

A redemption will qualify as an exchange under Section 302, therefore qualifying for sale or exchange treatment for income tax purposes, if any one of the following alternative requirements is met:

(1) If the redemption is not essentially equivalent to a dividend. Section 302(b)(1). Since the scope of this subjective requirement is unclear, it offers little help in advance planning for redemptions under a stock redemption agreement. The Supreme Court case of *United States v. Davis*, 397 U.S. 301 (1970), *rehearing denied*, 397 U.S. 1071 (1970), held that Section 302(b)(1) did not apply unless a meaningful reduction occurs in the stockholder's propor-

tionate interest in the corporation and that the existence of a business purpose for the redemption was irrelevant. However, in later revenue rulings, the IRS appears to have somewhat relaxed its strict interpretation of the *Davis* case, although the scope of these rulings, and their utility for advance planning, is unclear. *E.g.,* Rev. Ruls. 75-502, 1975-2 C.B. 111; 75-512, 1975-2 C.B. 112; 76-364, 1976-2 C.B. 91; and 76-385, 1976-2 C.B. 92.

(2) If the redemption is substantially disproportionate—that is, if after the redemption the stockholder owns less than 50% of the voting stock of the corporation *and* the percentage of the voting stock owned by the stockholder immediately after the redemption is less than 80% of the percentage of voting stock owned by him before the redemption. If the corporation has more than one class of stock outstanding, all of the common stock owned by the redeemed stockholder, both voting and nonvoting, must also comply with the 80% requirement. Section 302(b)(2).

> **Example:** A and B, two unrelated individuals, each own 50 shares of common stock of X Corp., all of its outstanding stock. X Corp. redeems 20 of A's shares. The redemption qualifies. A owns less than 50% of the voting stock after the redemption (30 shares/80 shares = 37½%). In addition, the percentage of A's voting stock after the redemption, 37½% (30 shares/80 shares), is less than 80% of the percentage of his voting stock before the redemption, 50% (50 shares/100 shares). [80% of A's percentage of voting stock before the redemption is 40% (80% of 50%), and his percentage of voting stock after the redemption, 37½%, is less than 40%].

From a planning point of view, a redemption that contemplates the reduction of a stockholder's interest from a majority or parity holding to a minority interest (as in the above Example) will usually not be advisable for the redeemed stockholder. Therefore, a stock redemption agreement will usually provide for the complete redemption of a stockholder's stock (except in the case of a Section 303 redemption), discussed below.

(3) If the redemption terminates the stockholder's stock interest in the corporation—that is, if all of his or her stock is completely redeemed by the corporation. Section 302(b)(3).

> **Example:** A and B, two unrelated individuals, each own 50 shares of the common stock of X Corp., all of its outstanding stock. The corporation redeems all of A's shares. The redemption qualifies for exchange treatment under Section 302(b)(3).

Section 302(b)(3), therefore, is usually the applicable provision that provides favorable tax treatment in the case of a complete redemption under the typical stock redemption agreement.

(4) If the redemption is in partial liquidation of the corporation. Section 302(b)(4). This provision generally requires a significant contraction of the corporation's business; it will, therefore, rarely apply to a redemption under a typical stock redemption agreement, because the purpose of the agreement is to permit the remaining or surviving stockholders to continue the very same corporate business that existed before the redemption.

C. The Section 318 Attribution Rules

Determining whether a redemption meets the Section 302 requirements is complicated by the constructive ownership rules of Section 318, commonly referred to as the "attribution rules." These rules are described in the table in Exhibit 2. Under the attribution rules, a stockholder is deemed to constructively own (in addition to the stock he or she actually owns) stock owned by specified related persons or entities. These rules are made applicable expressly to Section 302 redemptions (including Section 302(b)(1) redemptions). Section 302(c)(1); *United States v. Davis, supra*. The attribution rules do not, however, apply to a Section 303 redemption, discussed below.

   The attribution rules that most affect stock redemption agreements are the family attribution rules, Section 318(a)(1), and the estate-beneficiary and trust-beneficiary attribution rules, Sections 318(a)(3)(A) and (B). These rules can be illustrated by the following examples.

> **Example:** Family attribution rules: Father (F) and Son (S) each own 50 shares of common stock of X Corp., all of its outstanding stock. F's stock is completely redeemed. The redemption will not qualify. Under the family attribution rules, F will be deemed to constructively own his son's stock, and thus F will be deemed to own 100% of the stock of the corporation both before and after the redemption. (However, see the discussion of the waiver of the family attribution rules, below).
>
> **Example:** Estate beneficiary attribution rules: Father (F) and Son (S) each own 50 shares of common stock of X Corp. (all of its outstanding stock); S is a beneficiary under F's will. Under a stock redemption agreement, all of the stock of X Corp. owned by F's estate is to be redeemed at his death by the corporation. F dies, and the corporation redeems all of his stock from his estate. The redemption will not qualify. Under the estate beneficiary attribution rules, F's estate will be deemed to constructively own the estate beneficiary's stock (the stock of the son), and thus F's estate will be deemed to own 100% of the stock of the corporation both before and after the redemption.
>
> **Example:** Combination of trust beneficiary and estate beneficiary attribution rules—double attribution: Father (F) and Son (S) each own 50 shares of common stock of X Corp., all of its outstanding stock. F's will is a typical two-trust will, creating a marital trust and a residuary trust. (The marital trust could be a QTIP trust, and the residuary trust could be a unified credit trust.) Under the will, at the death of F's wife, the residuary trust is to be distributed to S. Under a stock redemption agreement, the stock of a stockholder is to be redeemed at his death. F dies and the corporation redeems his stock. The redemption will not qualify. Under the trust beneficiary attribution rules, the residuary trust will be deemed to constructively own the trust beneficiary's stock (the son's stock). Then, under the estate beneficiary attribution rules, F's estate will be deemed to constructively own the stock constructively owned by the estate beneficiary, which is the trust. Thus, F's estate will be deemed to own 100% of the stock of the corporation both before and after the redemption. The result in the foregoing example is double-attribution and is precisely what the Internal Revenue Service held in Rev. Ruls. 67-24, 1967-1 C.B. 75 and 71-261, 1971-1 C.B. 108. However, double-attribution will not occur in the case of certain "sideways" attributions. For example, stock attributed to one family member from a second family member will not be reattributed to a third family member, and stock attributed to

an estate from one beneficiary will not be reattributed from the estate to another estate beneficiary. Section 318(a)(5).

Section 302(c)(2) permits the waiver of the *family* attribution rules in determining whether a *termination of interest redemption* has occurred for purposes of Section 302(b)(3), if the following requirements are met:

(1) Immediately after the redemption, the redeemed stockholder must have no interest in the corporation (including an interest as an officer, director, or employee), other than as a creditor; he or she cannot serve as a corporate consultant, even if it is as an independent contractor (*Lynch v. Commissioner*, 83 T.C. 597 (1984), *rev'd*, 801 F.2d 1176 (9th Cir. 1986)), but he or she can receive deferred compensation from the corporation. Rev. Rul. 84-135, 1984-1 C.B. 80.

(2) The redeemed stockholder must not acquire any interest in the corporation (other than by bequest or inheritance) for a period of 10 years after the redemption. Consequently, the stock redeemed should not be pledged back to secure a corporate note given for the purchase price; other corporate assets should be used to secure the note. *See Lynch v. Commissioner*, *supra*, and Rev. Proc. 2007-3, Section 3.01(26), 2006-1 I.R.B. 122, (the current IRS ruling policy).

(3) The redeemed stockholder must attach a statement to his or her income tax return for the year of the redemption in which he or she agrees to notify the IRS if any interest in the corporation is acquired within the 10-year period. Section 302(c)(2)(A); Reg. Sec. 1.302-4.

However, the family attribution rules may not be waived if:

(4) The stock of the redeemed stockholder was acquired during the 10-year period prior to the redemption from a person whose stock would at the time of the redemption be attributed to the redeemed stockholder under any of the attribution rules of Section 318; or

(5) Another person owns stock at the time of the redemption which is attributable to the redeemed stockholder under Section 318; that person acquired stock from the redeemed stockholder within the 10-year period preceding the redemption; and that person's stock is not also redeemed at the same time as the redemption of the stock of the redeemed stockholder.

The limitation in (4), above, will not apply (and therefore the family attribution rules can be waived if rules (1), (2), and (3) above are followed) if the acquisition of stock by the redeemed stockholder did not have the avoidance of federal income tax as one of its principal purposes. Section 302(c)(2)(B). Likewise, the limitation in (5) above will not apply (and therefore the family attribution rules can be waived, again if rules (1), (2), and (3) above are followed) if the disposition of stock by the redeemed stockholder did not have the avoidance of federal income tax as one of its principal purposes. Section 302(c)(2)(B).

For purposes of both limitations in (4) and (5), above, "a transfer of stock by the transferor, within the 10-year period ending on the date of the distribution, to a person whose stock would be attributable to the transferor shall not be deemed to have as one of its principal purposes the avoidance of federal income tax merely because the transferee is in a lower income tax bracket than the transferor." Regulation Section 1.302-4(g).

Example: Father (F) and Son (S) each own 50 shares of common stock of X Corp., all of its outstanding stock. S acquired his stock 5 years ago by gift (or purchase) from F at the time S became active in the business. If F's stock is completely redeemed in compliance with rules (1), (2), and (3), above, this redemption will qualify. The family attribution rules are waived by F, S's stock is therefore not attributed to F, and the redemption qualifies as a termination of interest. The rule listed as (5) above does not apply. Even though S acquired his stock from F within 10 years of the redemption, the disposition of stock by F to S did not have tax avoidance as a principal purpose because S was active in the business when he acquired his stock.

See, e.g., Rev. Rul. 77-293, 1977-2 C.B. 91, Rev. Rul. 77-455, 1977-2 C.B. 93, and *Lynch v. Commissioner, supra.* The IRS ruling policy on the "non-tax avoidance purpose" test is set forth in Rev. Proc. 2007-3, above.

Section 302(c)(2) only permits waiver of the *family* attribution rules; this was made explicit by TEFRA 82, which made clarifying amendments to Section 302(c)(2). Prior to TEFRA, the IRS took the position that an *entity* (such as an estate or trust) could not waive the family attribution rules—only an individual stockholder (from whom the stock is redeemed) could waive family attribution. However, the Tax Court in the case of *Crawford v. Commissioner,* 59 T.C. 830 (1973), rejected the IRS's position. TEFRA codified the *Crawford* case, and entity waiver of intermediate family attribution is now permitted.

Example: Father (F) and Son (S) each own 50 shares of the common stock of X Corp., all of its outstanding stock. Under F's will, his wife, W (S's mother), is the sole beneficiary of F's estate; S is not a beneficiary of the estate. F dies, and the corporation redeems all of his stock from his estate. Under Section 302(c)(2)(C), as amended by TEFRA, the redemption will qualify as a termination of interest, provided the estate and W both comply with the waiver rules previously discussed.

The TEFRA amendments permit the estate to waive the intermediate family attribution from S (the son) to W (his mother) and, thus, to block the further attribution from W (as an estate beneficiary) to the estate.

The apparent liberalization of the attribution rules by the TEFRA amendments will, however, have very limited planning application—they will *only* apply when the surviving stockholders are *not* beneficiaries of the deceased stockholder's estate. Conversely, when the surviving stockholders *are* beneficiaries of the deceased stockholder's estate (the normal case), the Conference Committee Report to TEFRA makes it clear that the estate cannot waive the estate-beneficiary attribution rules that *directly* attribute the beneficiaries' stock to the estate; only intermediate family attribution can be waived. Thus, TEFRA overrules the case of *Rickey v. United States,* 592 F.2d 1251 (5th Cir. 1979), which had held that an estate could waive the estate-beneficiary attribution rules.

Example: Assume the same facts as in the prior example, except that both W and S are beneficiaries of F's estate. Here the stock redemption from F's estate will not qualify. Under the estate beneficiary attribution rules, F's estate will be deemed to constructively own the stock of S, and the estate cannot waive this direct attribution from beneficiary to estate. Thus, F's estate will be deemed to own 100% of the stock both before and after the redemption.

An attempt could be made to end the beneficiary status of S in F's estate *prior* to the redemption by first distributing to S his entire legacy. *See* Regulation Section 1.318-3(a). However, this will not work to eliminate the attribution from S to the estate when the estate retains a claim against S for unpaid death taxes or expenses (*Estate of Webber, Sr. v. United States*, 404 F.2d 411 (6th Cir. 1968)), or when S is a residuary legatee of the estate. Rev. Rul. 60-18, 1960-1 C.B. 145.

Finally, there is apparently a conflict in the Circuits as to whether family hostility will prevent application of the attribution rules. Compare *Robin Haft Trust v. Commissioner*, 510 F.2d 43 (1st Cir. 1975), in which the court found the existence of family hostility a mitigating factor in the application of the constructive ownership rules of Section 318, with *David Metzger Trust v. Commissioner*, 693 F.2d 459 (5th Cir. 1982), in which the court cited to the "plain language of the Code, a goal of a coherent tax policy, and the relevant precedents" (*United States v. Davis*, 397 U.S. 301 (1970), and *Rickey v. United States*, 592 F.2d 1251 (5th Cir. 1979)) for applying a strict application of Section 318, notwithstanding family discord.

As should be clear from the foregoing, the redemption rules of Section 302 are complex, especially with the overlay of the attribution rules of Section 318. Generally, because of the attribution rules, a stock redemption agreement *cannot* be used at death in a family-owned corporation (whether a C Corporation or an S Corporation that was formerly a C Corporation) that has earnings and profits without adverse dividend consequences to the selling estate or trust. Note again the potential effect of the 2003 Act on the importance of this issue: while the selling stockholder will not be able to recover his or her tax basis tax-free, the maximum federal income tax on dividends through 2010 is only 15%. A cross-purchase agreement, therefore, would normally be used to ensure favorable income tax results (that is, no gain or loss to the selling estate or trust if the sale is made at federal estate tax values). A significant exception to this general rule is a family corporation owned solely by brothers and sisters, because these family attribution rules do not apply to siblings. A similarly significant exception to this general rule is a situation in which the other family stockholders are *not* beneficiaries of the deceased stockholder's estate (or are only specific legatees, whose interests can be distributed prior to the redemption). A final significant exception is provided by Section 303, discussed below.

D. Section 303 Redemptions

Section 303 provides for a special type of income tax-"qualifying" redemption at the death of a stockholder. If the applicable requirements of Section 303 are met, a redemption will qualify as an exchange, generating capital—not dividend—treatment for the selling estate or trust, to the extent the redemption proceeds do not exceed the sum of the decedent's estate, inheritance, legacy, and succession taxes (plus interest), and funeral and administration expenses allowable as deductions for estate tax purposes. There is, however, no requirement that the redemption proceeds are actually used to pay such taxes or expenses.

In order to qualify under Section 303, a redemption must meet certain requirements. The most important of these from a tax-planning point of view is that the value of the deceased stockholder's stock must constitute more than 35% of the value of his or her adjusted gross estate (with aggregation permitted for 20% or more-owned corporations). Section 303(b)(2). In addition, the stock to be redeemed must be included in the deceased's gross estate for estate tax purposes (Section 303(a)); the stockholder from whom the stock is redeemed must be obligated to pay the qualifying death taxes and expenses in an amount equal to the redemption proceeds (even if they are not actually so used) (Section 303(b)(3)); and the redemption generally must occur within 3 years and 90 days after filing the deceased stockholder's estate tax return (Section 303(b)(1)).

Under the typical stock redemption agreement, it is unlikely that Section 303 would permit all of the deceased stockholder's stock in the corporation to be redeemed in a qualifying redemption, because the amount that can be redeemed is limited to the amount of death taxes and funeral and administration expenses. In fact, after ERTA 81, Section 303 redemptions generally have become less useful, because the availability of ERTA's increased unified credit and unlimited marital deduction (when the spouse survives and the unlimited marital deduction is available and is planned for) will eliminate federal estate tax liability in many estates. As a result, in such estates, Section 303 would only permit the redemption of an amount equal to the deceased stockholder's state death taxes (if any) and funeral and administration expenses. However, as discussed below, planning for the use of Section 303 at the surviving spouse's death in any marital deduction scenario may make sense. Finally, Section 303 is obviously inapplicable to lifetime redemptions.

Thus, Section 303 by itself does not usually solve the income tax problems raised by a redemption under a stock redemption agreement, and one must resort to the complicated rules of Section 302 (with the overlay of the Section 318 attribution rules), described above. Nevertheless, where the goal is preservation of the deceased stockholder's interest in the corporation for other family members rather than liquidation of that interest, a Section 303 redemption can serve a useful purpose. Assuming the unlimited marital deduction is used at the death of the first spouse to die, the estate tax will be payable at the death of the surviving spouse. Consequently, a Section 303 redemption at the death of the surviving spouse can provide the cash necessary to pay the tax (*if* the estate meets the Section 303 requirements at the time of the surviving spouse's death). Planning will thus have to be refocused on qualifying the *survivor's* estate for Section 303 treatment when the tax is postponed until his or her death.

In addition, a Section 303 redemption can be used in connection with a Section 6166 installment payment of estate tax—the threshold limits are identical. *See* Ltr. Rul. 9202020, approving a serial redemption designed to qualify under both Sections 303 and 6166. Finally, a Section 303 redemption (up to the limits imposed by the Section) can be—and often is—combined with a cross-purchase arrangement among the other family-member stockholders for the balance of the decedent's shares.

E. Redemptions Using Appreciated Property

As a general rule, a corporation that distributes appreciated property to a stockholder in redemption of his or her stock recognizes gain on the difference between the fair market value of the property and its adjusted basis. Section 311(b). This highlights the need for cash to carry out the redemption and, thus, the need for life insurance as the funding vehicle for the buy-sell arrangement.

F. Accumulated Earnings Tax Problems

The effect of life insurance purchased by a C Corporation to fund an insured stock redemption agreement under the accumulated earnings penalty tax is an unsettled area of the law; the accumulated earnings tax does not apply to an S Corporation. The relevant issue is whether the use of corporate earnings to pay premiums for life insurance that funds a stock redemption is the retention of those earnings for the reasonable needs of the business. This question has not been clearly answered by the courts.

If a corporation has accumulated earnings of less than $250,000 ($150,000 for certain professional service corporations) for the year, because of the minimum credit provided under Section 535(c), there will be no accumulated earnings tax problem in any event. Even when accumulated earnings exceed the minimum credit, there will be no penalty tax if the corporation can demonstrate that the accumulation is necessary for working capital or other business needs independent of the stock redemption.

Whether the retention of earnings to fund a future redemption serves "the reasonable needs of the business" depends on whether the redemption serves a corporate or stockholder purpose. Most commentators agree that accumulating earnings to redeem a minority (50% or less) stockholder will be treated more favorably than an accumulation to redeem a majority stockholder. The theory is that it is easier to establish a corporate business purpose for the redemption of a minority stockholder—the preservation of corporate harmony by the removal of the dissident minority. *See, e.g., Oman Constr. Co. v. Commissioner*, T.C. Memo 1965-325. Conversely, the redemption of a majority stockholder appears to be a stockholder (rather than a corporate) purpose. *See Ted Bates & Co., Inc. v. Commissioner*, T.C. Memo 1965-251.

It seems clearer that the accumulation of earnings to pay for "pure" key-person insurance *is* a reasonable need of the business (regardless of whether the insured is a minority or a majority stockholder, so long as he or she is "key"). Consequently, many practitioners do not make specific reference to the funding insurance in a stock redemption agreement, but merely designate the insurance as "key person" insurance.

Section 537(b) provides that the reasonable needs of the business include the amount needed (or reasonably anticipated to be needed) *in the year of the stockholder's death, or thereafter*, to accomplish a Section 303 redemption. Clearly, this limited Section offers no safe harbor for *pre-death* accumulations to fund a stock redemption (Section 303 or otherwise).

G. Effect of the Corporate Alternative Minimum Tax

The corporate alternative minimum tax (AMT) provided for in Section 55, added by TRA 86, represents an attempt by Congress to tax a corporation's economic income. The tax, which applies to C Corporations (but not to S Corporations), is a flat 20% tax, with a $40,000 floor (subject to a phase-out). TRA 86 expanded existing tax preferences and added significant new preferences and adjustments, including, for tax years before 1990, the business untaxed reported profits (BURP) adjustment, and for years after 1989, the adjusted current earnings (ACE) adjustment. Under both tests, both the increase in cash surrender values (in excess of premiums paid) and—more important—the excess of death benefits over booked cash values of corporate-owned life insurance (funding a redemption arrangement or otherwise) are preferences for purposes of the AMT.

For taxable years beginning after December 31, 1986, the old corporate add-on minimum tax (which initially came into law in 1969) was replaced by the AMT, which is similar in design to the individual alternative minimum tax—that is, it is truly an alternative tax; the taxpayer pays the higher of the regular income tax or the AMT. Alternative minimum taxable income (AMTI) is defined by Section 56 as regular corporate taxable income adjusted for changes in certain accounting methods, such as depreciation, and increased by certain tax preference items. Tentative minimum tax (TMT) is computed by applying a flat 20% tax rate to AMTI in excess of a $40,000 exemption (and reducing that calculation by any allowable foreign tax credit). The $40,000 exemption is phased out completely for corporations with AMTI in excess of $310,000, under Section 55(d)(2). Finally, TRA 86 limited the amount of net operating loss deductions and credits that can reduce AMT.

Under Section 56(g), for taxable years beginning after December 31, 1989, the BURP adjustment has been replaced with an adjustment equal to 75% of the difference between the corporation's adjusted current earnings (ACE) and its pre-adjustment AMTI. Based on a 20% flat rate (and ignoring the floor), this results in a 15% flat tax. Under the ACE test, for life insurance policies (during the insured's life), the increase in "income on the contract" (as defined in Section 7702(g)) in excess of that portion of premiums "attributable to insurance coverage" is specifically made an adjustment for this purpose. Section 56(g)(4)(B)(ii). Accordingly, during the insured's life, the adjustment for life insurance policies is, in effect, equal to the increase in cash value for the year minus the policy premium for that year, as it was under the prior BURP test.

In addition, as under the prior BURP test, at the insured's death, the excess of the policy death benefit (including for this purpose any policy loan deducted from the proceeds) over the corporation's adjusted basis in the policy for ACE purposes is also included in ACE. Accordingly, for AMT purposes, life insurance continues to be treated under the ACE test as it was under the BURP test. *See* Reg. Sec. 1.56(g)-1(c)(5), describing the application of the ACE rules to both the inside buildup and the death proceeds of life insurance contracts.

The Revenue Reconciliation Act of 1989 contained a provision that allowed any AMT generated by the ACE test to be considered a minimum tax credit that can be used to offset future regular corporate income tax (but not AMT). This continues the result under the prior BURP test that the AMT generated by the receipt of life insurance death proceeds would result in a timing, rather than a permanent, tax difference—assuming the corporation resumed paying regular tax. If regular corporate income tax is paid again in the future, the effect of the ACE adjustment on insurance death proceeds would only be a time value of money issue.

Finally, the 1997 Act exempts "small" C Corporations (as defined above) from this tax.

Accordingly, for an insured stock redemption agreement in a "large" C Corporation—but *not* for the insured cross-purchase agreement (even if funded under a split-dollar or loan arrangement with the corporation)—the corporate AMT in the year of the insured's death could be a major concern. The insured cross-purchase agreement will not create a corporate AMT problem, because the corporation is not receiving any insurance death benefits. Even if a split-dollar or loan arrangement were used to fund such an arrangement, the AMT usually will not be an issue, because the corporation is effectively only getting its money back for insurance premiums advanced and is not receiving any of the insurance death benefit gain. Because the AMT is a true alternative tax regime, its application to the death proceeds funding a redemption agreement will be unpredictable—it will depend on the corporation's other tax preferences and its regular tax-AMT posture in the year the insurance proceeds are collected.

The possible application of this tax has given some impetus to restructuring redemption agreements into cross-purchases (since the AMT isn't a risk there) and/or to electing S Corporation status (since the AMT only applies to C Corporations). For the redemption/cross-purchase switch, the major issue will likely be moving the insurance funding from the corporation to the co-stockholders of each insured—which raises both income tax and transfer-for-value issues, discussed in Chapter One. Alternatively, the switch to S Corporation status has other tax consequences that need to be taken into account, particularly in view of the increase of individual over corporate income tax rates after RRA 93, and the application of the built-in gains tax provisions of TRA 86. Perhaps the extension under the ACE test of the carry-forward of any AMT paid against future regular corporate income tax will lessen the incentive for considering these alternative strategies, as the effect will be only the loss of the use of the money paid in AMT (until the corporation resumes paying regular tax—assuming it does so), and the exemption of "small" C Corporations from the tax will take away any such incentive for such corporations.

The end result may well be that the theoretical imposition of AMT on corporate-owned life insurance will not pose a significant problem in practice; if it does in a particular case, the purchase of additional insurance to "fund" the payment of the AMT might be considered (taking into account the additional AMT exposure that such insurance would create—requiring a circular calculation to determine how much additional death benefit would be needed to fully fund the AMT cost).

Chapter Nine

S Corporation Concerns in Drafting Buy-Sell Agreements

A. In General

The S Corporation status of the corporate party can both complicate and simplify buy-sell agreements. The interplay of the S Corporation rules with the C Corporation rules adds more complexity, especially when the corporation previously had been a C Corporation. *See, e.g.,* Sections 291—corporate tax preference, 1362(d)(3)—passive investment income termination, 1363(d)—LIFO recapture, 1371(d)—investment credit recapture, 1374—built-in gain tax, and 1375—passive investment income tax rules. On the other hand, the S Corporation provisions often preclude application of C Corporation rules, thereby eliminating certain C Corporation issues (e.g., the accumulated earnings tax and the AMT).

Additionally, a buy-sell agreement that is prepared for an S Corporation should specifically address the concern that a transfer by one of the S Corporation stockholders could inadvertently terminate the corporation's S election, either because of the identity of the proposed transferee (e.g., a partnership, corporation, ineligible trust, or nonresident alien) or the number of stockholders after the transfer (the total number cannot exceed 100).

Specifically, no transfer should be permitted to an ineligible stockholder. Perhaps requiring an opinion of counsel to the effect that the proposed transfer would not terminate the Corporation's S election would be good practice, especially in light of the recent legislation that eases (or even eliminates) many of the prior S Corporation ownership restrictions. The agreement might also provide that violative transfers are to be void from inception and subject to injunctive relief in order to avoid S election termination, since monetary damages likely would not adequately compensate the innocent parties. Finally, purported transfers in violation of the agreement should not affect beneficial share ownership—a stockholder purporting to make such a transfer should continue to have dividend and any voting rights, and be required to report income or loss allocated pursuant to Section 1366.

In addition, a shareholders' agreement for an S Corporation can serve another important purpose. Because the stockholders are taxed on their proportionate share of S Corporation net income, whether or not distributed, minority stockholders should insist that the corporation be required to pay dividends after each taxable year at least equal to the sum of the maximum federal and applicable state individual income tax rates times the corporation's taxable income for the year. The maximum federal and applicable state individual income tax rates should be used—and not the applicable rate for each individual stockholder—to avoid a disparity in the distribution rights of each stockholder (based on their respective income tax rates) that could result in a prohibited second "class of stock," discussed below. Earlier payments could be considered (or insisted upon), in order to fund the stockholders' estimated tax payments.

One of the requirements to qualify as an S Corporation under Section 1361 is that the corporation not have more than one class of stock. The IRS issued final regulations concerning this single class of stock requirement on May 28, 1992. The final regulations provide that an S Corporation will be treated as having only one class of stock if all of the outstanding shares confer identical rights to distribution and liquidation proceeds. *See* Treas. Reg. § 1.1361-1(l). However, differences in voting rights among shares are disregarded for purposes of determining whether there is more than one class of stock.

Buy-sell agreements entered into or substantially modified after May 28, 1992, should be scrutinized to ensure that the agreement's provisions fall within one of the exceptions in the regulations and that the distribution or liquidation rights thereunder do not create a separate class of stock. The regulations provide that bona fide agreements to redeem or purchase stock at the time of death, divorce, disability, or termination of employment are disregarded in determining whether a corporation's shares confer identical rights; accordingly, an agreement conferring rights triggered upon one of these events will not be considered a second class of stock. Likewise, other restrictions imposed by the agreement (e.g., a restriction on the transfer of stock, or other redemption or purchase agreements not within the class mentioned above) will be disregarded in determining whether the corporation's stock confers identical rights to the shareholders unless: (1) a principal purpose of the agreement is to circumvent the one class of stock requirement, *and* (2) the agreement establishes a purchase price that, at the time the agreement is entered into, is significantly in excess of or below the fair market value of the stock. Reg. Section 1.1361-1(l)(2)(iii). See Chapter Six for a discussion of how such restrictions may similarly be disregarded for transfer tax purposes under Section 2703.

Based on the test set out above, the agreement may avoid all single class of stock issues if the purchase price provided in the agreement is book value or a price between fair market value and book value. An agreement providing for a price in this range is *not* considered to establish a price that is "significantly in excess of or below the fair market value of the stock" and is, therefore, disregarded in determining whether the outstanding shares confer identical rights. Reg. Sec. 1.1361-1(1)(2).

Finally, the Corporation's S status will have an effect on the choice of form of the stockholders' agreement.

B. Stock Redemption Agreements

The preference for exchange or distribution treatment will be affected by the corporation's relative accumulated adjustments account and accumulated earnings and profits account balances. If the redemption qualifies for Sections 302(a) or 303(a) exchange treatment, the corporation's accumulated adjustments account and accumulated earnings and profits account balances, if any, will be reduced in proportion to the percentage of stock redeemed to the total stock. Sections 1368(e)(1)(B) and 1371(c)(2). Surviving stockholders generally will want accumulated earnings and profits reductions (to reduce the taxable dividend potential of future distributions) but will want to avoid accumulated adjustments account reductions, as those amounts could be distributed tax-free.

For lifetime redemptions, exchange treatment for the redeemed stockholder generally will result in long-term capital gain treatment. The consequences of distribution treatment for the redeemed stockholder will depend on whether the corporation has accumulated earnings and profits. If it does not, the distribution is tax-free up to stock basis, and the balance is exchange gain. If the S Corporation has earnings and profits (accumulated while it was a C Corporation), the distribution is treated first as a return of stock basis and exchange gain to the extent of accumulated adjustments account, then as a dividend to the extent of the accumulated earnings and profits, and, finally, as return of stock basis or exchange gain for any remainder. Sections 1368 (b) and (c). Note again the effect of the 2003 Act, which provides that qualifying dividends will be taxed at a maximum federal rate of only 15% while that provision is in effect.

In post-mortem redemptions, the estate or other successor will prefer exchange treatment in order to utilize the Section 1014 tax-free basis step-up to preclude gain recognition (except for decedents dying in 2010). Distribution treatment will result in the same tax consequences as for similar lifetime redemptions, and the basis step up should eliminate any exchange gain.

The receipt of life insurance death proceeds funding a redemption generally will increase *all* the stockholders' bases in their shares, including, as noted above, those of the deceased stockholder's shares, which would have just received a Section 1014 step-up. In a cash basis corporation, to avoid "wasting" the Section 1014 step-up, if it is possible, the deceased stockholder's shares should be redeemed *before* the insurance proceeds are received (perhaps by use of a corporate note); the entire basis increase then will be allocated among surviving stockholders. If both steps are to occur in a single taxable year, a Section 1377(a)(2) closing of the books method election should be made as of the date of termination of the decedent's interest. This technique appears not to work in an accrual basis corporation, as its right to the insurance proceeds matures for tax purposes at the stockholder's death. *See* Ltr. Rul. 200409010.

C. Cross-Purchase Agreements

A stock purchase under a cross-purchase arrangement will not affect a corporation's accumulated adjustments account or accumulated earnings and profits directly, since the transaction does not involve the corporation. Thus, the surviving stockholders will have a larger accumulated adjustments account balance against which to receive future tax-free distributions, and they will also get a new cost basis in the stock they acquire.

The selling stockholder will be allocated income and loss on a per-share, per-day, basis, but unless a closing of the books election is made under I.R.C. Section 1377(a)(2), the amount of income earned by the corporation after the date of transfer may impact the amount of income the transferring shareholder must recognize. Gain on the sale generally will be exchange gain. For sales at death, the Section 1014 basis step-up precludes gain recognition (unless the stock's value increases between the date of death and the date of sale), but the income allocation and basis step-up can produce capital loss (which may not be fully used).

If the agreement is among non-employee stockholders and is funded with life insurance for which the corporation pays the premiums, the corporation will have a nondeductible expense, and the stockholders will be treated as receiving dividend distributions equal to their respective premium obligations. The same result would occur if the policies were arranged on a split-dollar basis, except that the measure of the income resulting from the distribution would be the "annual economic benefit." *See* Rev. Rul. 79-50, Notice 2002-8, and the final split-dollar regulations, discussed above. These distribution amounts may or may not be taxable to the stockholders, depending on the accumulated adjustments account, accumulated earnings and profits, if any, and the stockholders' respective stock bases.

Additionally, the distribution amounts will most likely not be in proportion to the stockholders' ownership percentages, in part because the respective premiums will differ. The IRS's single class of stock regulations can be read to treat such deemed distributions as nonconforming, thereby jeopardizing the S election. Treas. Reg. Section 1.1361-1(l)(2)(ii). While the regulations have been criticized, they could cast a shadow over corporate split-dollar funding of non-employee stockholder cross-purchase premiums in S Corporations, at least when the arrangement is non-contributory; with a contributory plan, as long as the contribution by the stockholder is equal to the deemed distribution (i.e., equal to the annual economic benefit), this should not be an issue. *See* Ltr. Ruls. 9318007 and 9331009. Note again that for post-final regulation arrangements, the contributions by the stockholders would be income to the corporation.

If the stockholders are also employees and the premium payments made by the corporation are received by them in their employee status, the single class of stock issue will not be a problem, as the regulations do not appear to apply to disproportionate compensation (as opposed to disproportionate dividend) distributions. *See* Ltr. Rul. 9248002, which held that an S Corporation's payments of policy premiums in excess of the term insurance cost (i.e., the annual economic benefit) on policies purchased and owned by employees and their spouses, under a split-dollar plan, would not violate the single class of stock requirement.

D. Summary

The impact of a corporation's status as an S Corporation on buy-sell planning can be summarized as follows:

1. For the non-insured buy-sell agreement, S Corporation status means that there are no Section 302/318 concerns in a redemption arrangement, even in a family context, *as long as* there are no accumulated earnings and profits from a prior C Corporation status, making a redemption more attractive, especially in a family business context.
2. For the insured buy-sell agreement, S Corporation status means that in a redemption arrangement, the possible partial increase in basis for the surviving stockholders (because of the tax-free receipt by the corporation of the insurance proceeds) and the inapplicability of the accumulated earnings tax and the AMT also make a redemption more attractive (despite the "wasted basis" issue, described above).
3. There is obviously no impact of the corporation's S status on a cross-purchase arrangement because of insurance funding (since the corporation won't pay any of the premiums or receive any of the policy death benefits).
4. Accordingly, the usual preference for a redemption arrangement is given added impetus in an S Corporation setting—especially when there are no prior C Corporation accumulated earnings and profits and the agreement is funded with life insurance.

5. Transfer restrictions, for transfers both during life and at death, will be more critical than in non-S Corporation agreements, even after the 1996 legislation, to prevent an inadvertent termination of the S election because shares are acquired by an ineligible stockholder.

For a more detailed analysis of insured buy-sell agreements in S Corporations, *see* WILLIAM D. KLEIN & DAVID C. BAHLS, INSURANCE COUNSELOR SERIES: S CORPORATIONS AND LIFE INSURANCE, 2d Ed. (ABA 2000).

Chapter Ten

Conclusion

The insured stock purchase agreement has proven to be an extremely successful tool for ensuring the harmonious continuation of the closely held corporation and solving the estate-planning problems of its stockholders. If properly drafted and funded, the agreement can accomplish the important aims of: (a) protecting the corporation and existing stockholders against unwanted new stockholders; (b) providing liquidity to a stockholder or his or her estate on a favorable income tax basis; (c) subject to the Section 2703 concerns discussed above, fixing the value of a stockholder's stock for death tax purposes; and (d) in the case of an S Corporation, ensuring continuation of the S election.

Exhibit 1
Comparison of Stock Redemption and Cross-Purchase Agreements

	Stock Redemption	Cross-Purchase
1. The Plan	The corporation contracts with the stockholders that upon a triggering event (e.g., a stockholder's death, disability, or termination of employment), the stock will be purchased by the corporation at an agreed-upon price.	The stockholders agree among themselves that the other stockholders will purchase the stock upon a triggering event at an agreed upon price.
2. Purchaser	The corporation.	The other stockholders.
3. Seller	The stockholder or his or her estate.	The stockholder or his or her estate.
4. Estate Tax Effects to Stockholder upon Sale at Death	If the estate is bound to sell, the agreed price may control for federal estate tax purposes (subject to § 2703 for intra-family agreements).	If the estate is bound to sell, the agreed price may control for federal estate tax purposes (again, subject to §2703 for intra-family agreements).
5. Tax Basis of Seller	The stock receives a stepped-up basis at the death of the deceased stockholder, but it will be "wasted" if the redemption is treated as a dividend.	The stock receives a stepped-up basis at the death of the deceased stockholder.
6. Basis of Purchased Stock for Other Stockholders	The surviving stockholders do not receive a new basis for the shares purchased, because the corporation is the purchaser. The value of their stock may be enhanced (as they own a greater percentage of the company), but their basis remains unchanged. Their lifetime sale of stock after a redemption results in more taxable gain to them. However, in an *insured* S Corporation redemption, the surviving stockholders *will receive* at least a partial increase in stock basis, to reflect the corporation's receipt of the tax-free insurance proceeds.	The purchasing stockholders receive a full, new basis for shares purchased from the decedent's estate. A subsequent lifetime sale will result in less taxable gain to them.
7. Life Insurance Funded	The corporation is the applicant, owner, premium payer, and beneficiary of a policy on the life of each stockholder in an amount sufficient to ensure performance of its purchase obligation under the agreement. The policy proceeds are received by the corporation income tax-free, subject to compliance with § 101(j).	Each stockholder is the applicant, owner, and beneficiary of a policy on the life of each of the other stockholders. Premiums are paid by the stockholders (unless subject to a split-dollar agreement). The policy proceeds are received by the stockholder income tax-free.

	Stock Redemption	Cross-Purchase
8. Number of Policies Needed	Only one policy per stockholder is required.	A larger number of policies is required; the formula for the number of policies needed is: n(n1), where n=the number of stockholders, unless one policy per stockholder is acquired by a partnership (or LLC) owned by the stockholders.
9. Premiums on Life Insurance	Premiums on life insurance to fund a stock redemption agreement are a nondeductible expense to the corporation. The increase in the policy's cash value is a corporate asset and is not considered a constructive dividend to the stockholders.	Premiums on life insurance to fund a cross purchase agreement are a non-deductible expense to the stockholders. Since premiums are paid by the stockholders, there is no constructive dividend problem. If the premiums are paid by the corporation under a split-dollar agreement, the value of each stockholder's annual economic benefit attributable to the policies insuring the other stockholders will either be contributed by the benefited stockholder or reported as income.
10. Comparative Tax Brackets	The premium payment by a high-tax-bracket corporation may be more costly than a deductible salary increase to the lower-bracket stockholders and their personal payment of the premiums under a cross-purchase arrangement.	The premium payment by lower bracket stockholders through a salary increase (deductible by the corporation) may be less expensive than if the corporation pays the premium. If a cross purchase agreement is funded by a split-dollar insurance arrangement, the economic and tax impact will be similar to a redemption arrangement.
11. Effect of Insurance on Value of Corporate Stock	Upon the death of an insured stockholder, the difference between the cash value and the policy proceeds is gain to the corporation on its financial statements, increasing the book value of the stock. This increase in value may or may not be included in the price under the agreement; if it is, the arrangement will be underfunded; if it is not, there may be § 2703 implications in a family setting.	Equity to all parties is achieved; the net worth of the corporation is unaffected by the receipt of the insurance proceeds by the other stockholders.

	Stock Redemption	Cross-Purchase
12. Value of Proceeds Includible in Estate of Decedent Stockholder	If all of the incidents of ownership for the policy are owned by the corporation, only the value of the stock, not the insurance, will be includible in the decedent's gross estate for estate tax purposes.	Although the value of the decedent's stock and the cash value of the policies owned by the decedent on the other stockholders' lives are includible in the decedent stockholder's estate, none of the proceeds of the policy(ies) on his or her life are included.
13. Percentage of Ownership in Corporation by Survivors after Triggering Event	The surviving stockholders' percentage of ownership is increased pro rata by the amount redeemed based upon their previous ownership ratios.	The surviving stockholders' percentage of ownership can remain the same or change depending upon the amount of the decedent's stock purchased by each survivor.
14. Effect on Family Corporation	When the stock is owned by "related" persons, redemption from the estate of a deceased stockholder's estate may result in unfavorable tax results (i.e., dividend treatment instead of sale or exchange treatment) to the estate through the application of the § 318 attribution and constructive ownership rules. This problem may be solved if the redemption qualifies under § 303 or in an S Corporation with no C Corporation accumulated E & P.	There are no problems of constructive ownership or attribution under §318 when the stock is purchased by the stockholders, rather than the corporation.
15. Changing Agreement to the Other Form	The transfer of the policies from the corporation to the stockholders may create transfer-for-value and income issues for the stockholders.	Transferring the policies from the stockholders to the corporation will not create transfer for value or income realization problems. Accordingly, it may be easier to start with a cross purchase agreement.

	Stock Redemption	Cross-Purchase
16. Transfer of Policies	The transfer of policies to the surviving stockholders at the death of one stockholder is not necessary. Accordingly, there is no transfer-for-value problem at that time.	The estate of the deceased stockholder will own policies on the lives of the surviving stockholders. To provide for full funding upon a subsequent death, the estate must transfer these policies to the survivors; however, to avoid a transfer for value problem for the surviving stockholders, the estate can only sell the policies to: the respective insureds; the corporation (when the insured is an officer or stockholder); a partnership in which the insured is a partner; or a partner of the insured. The use of a partnership (or LLC) to own one policy on each stockholder would avoid this issue.
17. Corporate Law Compliance	The applicable state's corporation code may require that the purchase by the corporation be made only out of "surplus."	No such restrictions.
18. Claims of Creditors	The policy proceeds and the cash value of corporate-owned life insurance are usually subject to the claims of the corporation's creditors, subject to any exemptions provided for life insurance under state law.	Because the policies are owned by the individual stockholders, corporate creditors cannot reach the proceeds or cash value of these non-corporate assets. However, the individual owner's creditors could reach the policies, again subject to any state law exemption for insurance.

Exhibit 2
Rules of Attribution

The table below illustrates the relationships and effects of the Rules of Attribution of I.R.C. Sec. 318 to Corporate Stock Redemptions under I.R.C. Sec. 302.

Attributed from	Attributed to	Basis of Attribution	Code Sections
1. Family Members: Spouse, not legally separated Parents Children Grandchildren Adopted Children	Family Members, but not between siblings or to grandchildren from grandparents	Entire interest	318(a)(1)(A) and (B)
2. Partnership Estate	Partners Beneficiaries	Proportionately	318(a)(2)(A)
3. Nongrantor Trust	Beneficiaries	In proportion to actuarially computed interest	318(a)(2)(B)(i)
4. Grantor Trust (I.R.C. Secs. 671-679)	Grantor or other person considered the owner	Entire interest	318(a)(2)(B)(ii)
5. Corporation	Stockholder owning 50% or more in value of the corporation's stock	In proportion to the value the stock owned by such stockholder bears to the value of all stock in the corporation	318(a)(2)(C)
6. Partner Beneficiary	Partnership Estate	Entire interest	318(a)(3)(A)
7. Beneficiary—unless the beneficiary's interest is a remote contingent interest (actuarially 5% or less of the value of the trust property)	Nongrantor Trust	Entire interest	318(a)(3)(B)(i)
8. Grantor or other person considered owner of a Grantor Trust (I.R.C. Secs. 671-679)	Grantor Trust	Entire interest	318(a)(3)(B)(ii)

Attributed from	Attributed to	Basis of Attribution	Code Sections
9. Stockholder owning 50% or more in value of a corporation's stock	Corporation	Entire interest	318(a)(3)(C)
10. Stock Option	Person holding the option	Stock subject to the option	318(a)(4)

NOTE: This table does not illustrate "double attribution" pitfalls, I.R.C. Sec. 318(a)(5), or "waiver" of the family attribution rules (Rule 1 above) in termination of interest redemptions, I.R.C. Sec. 302(c)(2). See Chapter Eight for a discussion of these issues.

(Adapted, with permission, from "Sale or Retention of the Closely Held Corporation," Study Outline published by the American Society of CLU & ChFC—now out of print.)

Exhibit 3

**SAMPLE FORM
STOCKHOLDERS AGREEMENT
FOR USE BY CLIENT'S ATTORNEY
DRAFTER'S NOTES**

1. Prohibits transfers during life except to some trusts and to certain donees; all provisions relating to donees allowed as stockholders appear in brackets. Generally, treats shares held by donees as held by the donor, for purposes of further transfers and sales.
2. Restricts both voluntary transfers during life as well as involuntary transfers (such as in a bankruptcy).
3. Drafted to allow for either cross-purchase or redemption arrangements; cross purchase and redemption provisions have all been shown as alternatives.
4. Provides for an agreed value purchase price for transfers at death (or an alternative using adjusted book value). Note the Code Section 2703 issue for family businesses raised by the determination of the purchase price; the agreed price will not "fix" estate tax values for the shares unless the agreed price is fair market value, determined without regard to the terms of the Agreement.
5. Contains optional provisions relating to the corporation's S Corporation status, designed to prevent unintentional termination of the election by a proposed transfer of shares to an ineligible stockholder.
6. Assumes all initial stockholders are individuals or wholly revocable trusts; must be edited where any stockholders are other trusts or are entities.

The sample Stockholders Agreement and other forms included in this volume are provided for the reference of the drafting attorney as an educational aid in drafting a particular client's document(s). The authors and the publishers hereby expressly disclaim any liability for the use of any of the sample agreements, the forms or any of the other materials contained in this volume, and expressly state that no express or implied warranty is made as to the effectiveness, validity or suitability of the forms or any other material contained herein for tax or legal purposes. The drafting lawyer is cautioned both that the sample agreements, forms and other materials contained herein have been prepared with an emphasis on general federal tax law; accordingly, they may not be appropriate to the state law requirements of any particular state, since federal tax law changes constantly, a current knowledge of federal income and transfer tax law is required at the time a particular client's Stockholders Agreement is planned and drafted. As always, the drafting lawyer is responsible for making all necessary modifications to the sample agreement(s) and other form(s) to make their use appropriate to the client's situation and to assure compliance with both then-current federal tax law and applicable state law.

STOCKHOLDERS AGREEMENT
OF
CORPORATION NAME

Table of Contents

CORPORATION NAME
STOCKHOLDERS AGREEMENT

This Stockholders Agreement, made and entered into this ____ day of _____, _____, by and among [Corporation Name], a _____ corporation, with principal offices and place of business in the City of _____, State of _____ (hereinafter referred to as the "Corporation"), and [Stockholder1], [Stockholder2], and [Stockholder3], all individuals residing in the State of _____ (hereinafter sometimes referred to collectively as the "Stockholders" and sometimes referred to individually as a "Stockholder").

WHEREAS, the Stockholders are the owners of all of the issued and outstanding shares of capital stock of the Corporation; and

WHEREAS, the parties hereto believe that it will be in their best separate and mutual interests if the sale and other transfer of shares of the capital stock of the Corporation is restricted, so that such shares continue to be closely held by persons active in the Corporation's business or certain revocable trusts created by them for their benefit during their respective lifetimes [or their donees] and are not distributed generally; and

WHEREAS, each Stockholder wishes to provide the terms and conditions under which the Stockholder's estate or the Stockholder's revocable trust [and the Stockholder's donees] will dispose of the shares of the capital stock of the Corporation owned by the Stockholder or the Stockholder's revocable trust [and the Stockholder's donees] at the Stockholder's death; and

[WHEREAS, each Stockholder wishes to have the first option to repurchase the shares of the capital stock of the Corporation owned by the Stockholder's donees, if any such donee wishes to dispose of such shares during the Stockholder's lifetime and to repurchase such shares owned by the estate of any such donee who dies during the lifetime of such Stockholder; and]

[CROSS PURCHASE ALTERNATIVE]
WHEREAS, each Stockholder has purchased or may purchase insurance policies insuring the life of each other Stockholder in order to provide all or a portion of the funds necessary to acquire the shares of the capital stock of the Corporation owned by each other Stockholder and each such other Stockholder's revocable trust [and each such other Stockholder's donees] at each such other Stockholder's death; and

[REDEMPTION ALTERNATIVE]
WHEREAS, the Corporation has purchased or may purchase insurance policies insuring the life of each Stockholder, the proceeds of which are payable to the Corporation, in order to provide all or a portion of the funds necessary for the Corporation to acquire its shares of capital stock owned by the estate of each Stockholder and such Stockholder's revocable trust [and the Stockholder's donees] at the Stockholder's death; and

[S CORPORATION OPTION]

WHEREAS, the Stockholders wish that, unless they unanimously agree otherwise, the Corporation shall remain an S Corporation, for federal income tax purposes, as provided for and defined by Subchapter S of Chapter 1 of Subtitle A of the Internal Revenue Code of 1986, as amended;

NOW, THEREFORE, in consideration of the premises, and of the mutual promises contained herein, the parties hereto agree as follows:

1. **Shares to Which Applicable**.

(a) The terms and conditions of this Stockholders Agreement shall apply to all Restricted Shares.

(b) Each Stockholder hereby represents and warrants with respect to the Restricted Shares heretofore issued to the Stockholder or a Permitted Trust created by such Stockholder that the Stockholder is the true and beneficial owner of the Restricted Shares issued to the Stockholder in the Stockholder's name, and such Trust is the true and beneficial owner of the Restrictive Shares issued in the name of such Trust, that no other person or entity has any ownership in such shares, and that such shares are owned by the Stockholder, or such Trust, free and clear of all liens and encumbrances.

(c) Ownership of Restricted Shares by a Permitted Trust shall be treated, for all purposes of this Agreement, as ownership of such shares by the Stockholder who is the grantor of such trust.

2. **Disposition During Life**.
  2.1. **Restriction on Transfer of Shares**.

Except with respect to a transfer permitted under Section 2.6, no Stockholder, during the Stockholder's lifetime, shall sell, assign, transfer, exchange, convey, hypothecate or otherwise dispose of any Restricted Shares, by sale, exchange, gift, operation of law or otherwise, without first: (i) giving a Notice of Proposed Transfer to the Corporation and to each other Stockholder, indicating that the Proposed Transferor intends to so transfer or dispose of any such Restricted Shares; and (ii) complying with all other terms of this Stockholders Agreement.

  (a) **Notice of Proposed Transfer**.

A Notice of Proposed Transfer required hereunder shall set forth the name or names of the proposed transferees, the manner by which the proposed transfer or other disposition of the Restricted Shares is to be effected, and the terms thereof, including, without limitation, the proposed purchase price, if any, and the terms of payment thereof. Any such Notice shall be given as required by Section 14.4. The Proposed Transferor shall represent and warrant the terms set forth in such Notice of Proposed Transfer to be the terms of a bona fide, valid and existing third party offer to purchase such Restricted Shares or the terms of a then contemplated disposition of such Restricted Shares by mortgage, pledge, gift, operation of law or otherwise, as the case may be.

  (b) **Right of First Refusal**.
    (1) **Terms and Purchase Price**.

The Notice of Proposed Transfer shall constitute an irrevocable offer by the Proposed Transferor first to the other Stockholders, and then to the Corporation, respectively, to purchase all of the Restricted Shares owned by the Proposed Transferor [and such Stockholder's Donees] (regardless of whether such Notice of Proposed Transfer relates to all such shares), on the terms and conditions provided therein, and for the purchase price per share which shall be the lower of: (i) the [Adjusted Book Value thereof as of the end of the Corporation's most recent annual accounting period ended prior to the date of such Notice of Proposed Transfer][Appraisal Value][Agreed Value], or (ii) the purchase price per share as specified in such Notice of Proposed Transfer. If the purchase price specified in such Notice of Proposed Transfer is not stated on a per share basis, the necessary adjustment to so specify such purchase price shall be made. If the proposed transfer is other than in exchange for valuable consideration which can be valued in money or money's worth, the purchase price per share in all instances shall be the Adjusted Book Value thereof.

    (2) **Exercise of Option**.

        (A) For sixty (60) days following the giving of such Notice of Proposed Transfer, each of the Stockholders (other than the Proposed Transferor) shall have the Ratable Option, hereby granted, to purchase all or any part of the Restricted Shares of the Proposed Transferor [and the Stockholder's Donees], at the price and on the terms and conditions set forth in Section 2.1(b) hereof. Such option shall be exercised by each such Stockholder by the giving of written notice of such exercise to the Proposed Transferor [and the Stockholder's Donees] within such sixty (60) day period.

        (B) If any of such Stockholders fails to exercise the Stockholder's Ratable Option to purchase such Restricted Shares, then each Stockholder who did exercise such Ratable Option shall have the further Ratable Option(s), hereby granted, to purchase such unpurchased Restricted Shares, such further Ratable Option(s) arising until any such Restricted Shares which remain unpurchased have been offered to each Stockholder who has exercised such Ratable Option(s). Each such further Ratable Option shall be exercisable for the five (5) day period beginning on the day immediately following the termination of the previous Ratable Option.

        (C) If all of the other Stockholders fail to fully exercise their respective options to purchase any such Restricted Shares within the time period provided herein, then, for thirty (30) days thereafter, the Corporation shall have the option, hereby granted, to purchase any such Restricted Shares not purchased by the Stockholders. Such option shall be exercised by the Corporation by giving written notice thereof to the Proposed Transferor [and the Stockholder's Donees] within such thirty (30) day period.

    (3) **Disposition of Shares Permitted If Options Not Exercised**.

        (A) In the event that the options hereinabove granted have not been exercised with respect to all Restricted Shares owned by the Proposed Transferor, then at the expiration of the time period provided herein, the Proposed Transferor [, but not the Stockholder's Donees,] may, within sixty (60) days thereafter, transfer or otherwise dispose of the same, at the price and on the terms set forth in such Notice of Proposed Transfer.

        (B) Any Restricted Shares so transferred or disposed of by the Proposed Transferor pursuant hereto shall continue to be subject to the restrictive provisions contained in this Stockholders Agreement in the hands of the transferee or transferees thereof. Any acceptance of such Restricted Shares subject hereto by any such transferee shall be deemed to be such transferee's agreement to be bound by all of the terms and conditions of this Stockholders Agreement. Each such transferee shall, as a condition of the transfer of such Restricted Shares to such transferee on the books of the Corporation, execute and deliver a supplemental agreement accepting the terms, conditions, and restrictive provisions of this Stockholders Agreement.

(C) If such Restricted Shares are not so transferred or disposed of by the Proposed Transferor pursuant hereto, then such Restricted Shares shall continue to be subject to all of the terms, conditions, and restrictive provisions of this Stockholders Agreement in the hands of the Proposed Transferor, and may not be transferred nor disposed of by the Stockholder thereafter, except in compliance with the terms, conditions and restrictive provisions of this Stockholders Agreement.

2.2. **Pledges and Other Encumbrances of Shares**.

(a) No Stockholder shall pledge, mortgage, or otherwise encumber any of the Stockholder's Restricted Shares without the prior written consent of the Corporation and of all the other Stockholders.

(b) Notwithstanding the foregoing, a Stockholder or the Stockholder's successor in interest may pledge, mortgage, or otherwise encumber any of the Stockholder's Restricted Shares, without first obtaining the written consent of the Corporation and all the other Stockholders, if (i) the pledgee is a bona fide lending institution; (ii) the purpose of the pledge, mortgage, or encumbrance is to obtain funds with which to pay federal or state estate, inheritance, or other transfer taxes (or interest or penalties thereon) imposed by virtue of the death of a Stockholder; and (iii) such funds are actually used for that purpose.

(c) If the Corporation and the other Stockholders consent in writing to any pledge, mortgage, or other encumbrance of a Stockholder's Restricted Shares, or if, pursuant to the provisions of Section 2.2(b) hereof, a Stockholder's Restricted Shares are pledged, mortgaged, or otherwise encumbered to provide funds for the payment of federal or state transfer taxes imposed by reason of the death of a Stockholder, the pledgee or pledgees shall, as a condition to the pledge, mortgage, or other encumbrance, agree in writing to (i) abide and be bound by all the terms, conditions, and restrictive provisions of this Stockholders Agreement as though the pledgee were a Stockholder, and (ii) exercise the pledgee's rights with respect to the Restricted Shares pledged, mortgaged, or otherwise encumbered only in accordance with this Agreement.

2.3. **Insolvency or Bankruptcy of a Stockholder or an Involuntary Transfer of Shares**.

Upon the occurrence of any of the following events with respect to any Stockholder, the other Stockholders and the Corporation shall respectively have the option to purchase all of the affected Stockholder's Restricted Shares (whether or not all such Restricted Shares are affected by such event) [and all of the Restricted Shares of such Stockholder's Donees], for the [Adjusted Book][Appraisal][Agreed] Value thereof, on the terms and conditions provided for herein as if the affected Stockholder had given the other Stockholders and the Corporation a Notice of Proposed Transfer indicating the Stockholder's intention to transfer or dispose of the Stockholder's Restricted Shares:

(a) any Stockholder shall be adjudicated a bankrupt or shall make an assignment for the benefit of the Stockholder's creditors;

(b) bankruptcy, insolvency, reorganization, debt arrangement or adjustment, liquidation or receivership proceedings in which any Stockholder is alleged to be insolvent or unable to pay the Stockholder's debts as they mature are instituted by or against such Stockholder (and, if instituted against such Stockholder, such Stockholder shall consent thereto or shall admit in writing the material allegations of the petition filed in said proceedings or said proceedings shall remain undismissed for sixty (60) days);

(c) any Restricted Shares of any Stockholder are attached or any judgment is obtained in any legal or equitable proceeding against any Stockholder and the sale of any of the Stockholder's Restricted Shares is contemplated or threatened under legal process as a result of judgment therein;

(d) any execution process is issued against any Stockholder by which any of the Stockholder's Restricted Shares may be voluntarily or involuntarily sold; or

(e) any judicial order is entered or any agreement is entered into which, in either case, would require a transfer of any of the Restricted Shares of any Stockholder to anyone not a party hereto (including but not limited to, a property division or settlement agreement in conjunction with a divorce proceeding, dissolution of marriage or legal separation).

2.4. **Disability of a Stockholder**.

(a) If any Stockholder who is an employee of the corporation ceases to be employed by the Corporation by reason of the Stockholder's Disability, the Corporation shall have the option to purchase all, but not less than all, of the Restricted Shares owned by such Stockholder [and the Stockholder's Donees] for the [Adjusted Book Value][Appraised Value][Agreed Value] thereof as of the end of the Corporation's most recent annual accounting period ended prior to the effective date of such Disability]. Such option shall be exercisable at any time during the 90-day period immediately after the expiration of six (6) months from the termination of such employment.

(b) If a Stockholder who is an employee of the Corporation ceases to be employed by the Corporation because of the Stockholder's Disability, such Stockholder shall have the right and option, exercisable by the Stockholder at any time after the expiration of eighteen (18) months after the termination of such employment, to require the Corporation to purchase all, but not less than all, of the Restricted Shares owned by the Stockholder [and the Stockholder's Donees] for the [Adjusted Book Value] [Appraised Value][Agreed Value] thereof as of the end of the Corporation's most recent annual accounting period ended prior to the effective date of such termination.

2.5. **Termination of Employment of a Stockholder**.

(a) If any Stockholder who is an employee of the corporation ceases to be employed by the Corporation for any reason (other than the Stockholder's death or Disability), whether voluntary termination of employment, discharge with or without cause, retirement, or any other cause whatsoever, the Corporation shall have the option to purchase all, but not less than all, of the Restricted Shares owned by such Stockholder [and the Stockholder's Donees] for the [Adjusted Book Value] [Appraised Value][Agreed Value]thereof as of the end of the Corporation's most recent annual accounting period ended prior to the effective date of the termination of the Stockholder's employment. Such option shall be exercisable by the Corporation at any time during the 90-day period immediately after the effective date of such termination of employment.

(b) [OPTIONAL] If a Stockholder who is an employee of the Corporation ceases to be employed by the Corporation for any reason (other than the Stockholder's death or Disability), such Stockholder shall have the right and option, exercisable by the Stockholder at any time for one hundred twenty (120) days after the expiration of ninety (90) days after the termination of such employment, to require the Corporation to purchase all, but not less than all, of the Restricted Shares owned by the Stockholder [and the Stockholder's Donees] for the [Adjusted Book Value] [Appraised Value][Agreed Value] thereof as of the end of the Corporation's most recent annual accounting period ended prior to the effective date of such termination.

2.6. **Permitted Transfers**.

Notwithstanding any other provision of this Stockholders Agreement to the contrary, a Stockholder shall have the right to transfer all or a portion of such Stockholder's Restricted Shares without having to give the Corporation and the other Stockholders a Notice of Proposed Transfer, to the transferees described in this Section 2.6.

(a) **Transfer to a Permitted Trust**.

Notwithstanding any other provision of this Stockholders Agreement, any Stockholder may transfer by gift, and without consideration, any part, or all of such Stockholder's Restricted Shares to a permitted Trust, without first offering such Restricted Shares to the Corporation or the other Stockholders hereunder.

(b) **[Permitted Gifts to Donees**. *(Optional)*

Notwithstanding any other provision of this Stockholders Agreement, any Stockholder may transfer, by gift, and without consideration, any part, or all, of such Stockholder's Restricted Shares to a Donee without first offering such Restricted Shares to the other Stockholders or the Corporation hereunder, on the condition that such Donee agrees, in writing, to be bound in every respect by the terms and conditions of this Stockholders Agreement as if such Donee were a Stockholder party hereto. The following terms and conditions shall apply only to Donees and shall, to the extent inconsistent with any other provision hereof, take precedence over such provision and shall prevail as to Donees:

(1) the terms and conditions of Section 2.1 shall apply to Donees, with the following modifications: (i) a Donee may transfer, by gift and without consideration, any part or all of such Donee's Restricted Shares to such Donee's donor Stockholder without first offering such Restricted Shares to the other Stockholders or the Corporation hereunder; (ii) no Donee may transfer any part of such Donee's Restricted Shares to a further donee other than his donor Stockholder; and (iii) the donor Stockholder of such Donee shall have the first option to purchase the Restricted Shares of a Donee intending to transfer or dispose of such Donee's Restricted Shares before such option is granted to the other Stockholders or the Corporation hereunder;

(2) all of the terms and conditions of Sections 2.3 and 2.4 shall apply to Donees, except that, upon the occurrence of any such event, the donor Stockholder of such Donee shall have the first option (on the same terms and conditions) to purchase the Restricted Shares of such Donee before such option is granted to the other Stockholders or the Corporation hereunder, as the case may be;

(3) all of the terms and conditions of Section 3, shall apply to Donees, except that, upon the death of a Donee, the donor Stockholder of such Donee shall have the first option (on the same terms and conditions) to purchase the Restricted Shares owned by such Donee at the time of such Donee's death before such option is granted to the other Stockholders or the Corporation hereunder, as the case may be; and

(4) none of the options granted herein to Stockholders to purchase Restricted Shares shall be applicable to nor exercisable by Donees.]

3. **Purchase at Death by Surviving Stockholders**. *(For Cross Purchase)*

Upon the death of any Stockholder (or upon the death of the grantor of a Permitted Trust which is a Stockholder), the surviving Stockholders shall ratably purchase, and the Representative of the deceased Stockholder or the trustee of any Permitted Trust shall sell, all of the Restricted Shares owned by such deceased Stockholder (or such grantor of a Permitted Trust which is a Stockholder) or Permitted Trust at the time of the Stockholder's death, [and the Donees of such deceased Stockholder shall sell all of the Restricted Shares owned by such Donees,] on the terms and conditions and for the price per share provided herein.

3.1. **Purchase Price**.

(a) The purchase price per share to be paid for any Restricted Shares purchased upon the death of a deceased Stockholder (or grantor of a Permitted Trust which is a Stockholder) shall be the [Adjusted Book] [Agreed] [Appraised] Value thereof.

(b) *(Optional)* Notwithstanding the foregoing, in the event that Restricted Shares are sold by the Corporation and/or the other Stockholders, within ___ months of the purchase of such deceased Stockholder's Restrictive Shares pursuant to the provisions of this subparagraph, at a per share price greater than the per share price received by the Representative of the deceased stockholder or Trustee of any Permitted Trust, such Representative or Trustee shall be entitled to receive the pro rata share of such subsequent sale as if such Representative or Trustee still owned such Restricted Shares.

4. **Redemption At Death by Corporation**. *(For Redemption)*

Upon the death of any Stockholder (or upon the death of a Stockholder who is the grantor of a Permitted Trust which is a Stockholder), the Corporation shall redeem, and the Representative of the deceased Stockholder or the trustee of any Permitted Trust shall offer for redemption, all of the Restricted Shares owned by such deceased Stockholder (or such deceased grantor of a Permitted Trust which is a Stockholder) or trust at the time of the Stockholder's death, [and the Donees of such deceased Stockholder shall offer for redemption all of the Restricted Shares owned by such Donees,] on the terms and conditions and for the price per share provided herein.

4.1. **Purchase Price**.

(a) The purchase price per share to be paid for any Restricted Shares purchased upon the death of a deceased Stockholder (or grantor of a Permitted Trust which is a Stockholder) shall be the [Adjusted Book] [Agreed] [Appraised] Value thereof.

(b) Notwithstanding the foregoing, in the event that shares of the capital stock or substantially all of the assets of the Corporation are sold by the Corporation and/or the other Stockholders, within ___ months of the redemption of such deceased Stockholder's Restrictive Shares pursuant to the provisions of this subparagraph, at a per share price greater than the per share price received by the Representative of the deceased stockholder or Trustee of a Permitted Trust [or a Donee of a deceased Stockholder hereunder], such representative or Trustee, as the case may be, shall be entitled to receive the pro rata share of such subsequent sale as if such representative or Trustee still owned such restrictive shares.

4.2. **Availability of Corporate Surplus**.

If, at the time it is required to redeem the Restricted Shares offered for redemption by the Representative of a deceased Stockholder or the trustee of any Permitted Trust [or a Donee of a deceased Stockholder hereunder], the Corporation shall not have sufficient surplus to permit it to lawfully purchase all of such Restricted Shares, the surviving Stockholders, [and] the Representative of such deceased Stockholder and the trustee of any Permitted Trust [and the Donees of such deceased Stockholder] shall promptly vote their respective holdings of shares of stock of the Corporation so as to reduce the capital of the Corporation, and shall take such other steps as stockholders of the Corporation as may be necessary in order to enable the Corporation to lawfully purchase and pay for all of the Restricted Shares which it is obligated to redeem hereunder.

5.   **Closing and Payment of Purchase Price**.
5.1. **Payment Terms and Installment Note**.

The aggregate purchase price for Restricted Shares purchased hereunder ("Purchase Price") shall be paid in full in cash or by bank, cashier's or certified check delivered to the selling Stockholder or the Stockholder's successor, as the case may be, on the closing date of such purchase; provided however, at the option of the purchaser, the Purchase Price payable in any case other than a purchase on payment terms set forth in a Notice of Proposed Transfer, may be paid in installments as follows:

(a) When a purchaser elects to purchase Restricted Shares in installments, the Purchase Price may be paid by a _____ Percent (___%) cash down payment at the closing of such purchase, and the balance in _____ (___) equal monthly installments.

(b) Such installments shall be represented by a promissory note (the "Note"), to be duly executed, dated and delivered by the purchaser on the closing date, in an original principal amount equal to the unpaid balance of the Purchase Price, together with interest at the Prime Rate on the outstanding principal balance.

(c) The purchaser will pay principal and interest on the Note starting one month following the closing date and thereafter for the _____ (___) succeeding months. The purchaser's final payment shall include all remaining principal and all accrued unpaid interest on the Note.

(d) The Note shall be prepayable, from time to time, in whole or in part, at the option of the purchaser, without penalty or premium.

(e) The Note shall be secured by the collateral pledge of all of the Restricted Shares being purchased.

5.2. **Application of Insurance Proceeds**.

(a) Notwithstanding any other provision hereof, if at the death of a Stockholder (or the death of a grantor of a Permitted Trust which is a Stockholder) the purchaser of Restricted Shares hereunder shall be entitled to collect any proceeds of any policy of insurance insuring the life of the deceased Stockholder (or grantor of a trust which is a Stockholder) whose Restricted Shares are being purchased hereunder, then, at the election of the Representative of such deceased Stockholder or the trustee of a Permitted Trust, as the case may be, the purchaser shall pay such proceeds on collection thereof to such Representative or trustee, as the case may be, at the closing of the purchase of such deceased Stockholder's Restricted Shares hereunder, as a credit against, and to the extent of, the Purchase Price thereof.

(b) If the entire amount of such proceeds is less than the Purchase Price of such Restricted Shares, the payment of such proceeds by the purchaser shall constitute the initial installment of the Purchase Price payable hereunder. If the entire amount of such proceeds collected by the purchaser is in excess of the Purchase Price of such Restricted Shares, such excess shall belong to the purchaser solely and absolutely, free from the terms of this Stockholders Agreement.

5.3. **Terms of Closing**.
 (a) **Location of Closing**.
The closing of any purchase of Restricted Shares hereunder shall be held at the principal office of the Corporation, or such other mutually convenient place as may be designated by the parties to such purchase.
 (b) **Time of Closing**.
With respect to a purchase of Restricted Shares during the lifetime of a Stockholder, such closing shall take place within ninety (90) days of the exercise of the last exercised option and/or Ratable Option to purchase such Restricted Shares by the other Stockholders or the Corporation, as provided herein. With respect to a purchase of Restricted Shares by reason of the death of any Stockholder, such closing shall take place within ninety (90) days after the appointment of the Representative of such deceased Stockholder, or within one hundred eighty (180) days after the death of such deceased Stockholder, if no such Representative has been appointed within said one hundred eighty (180) day period.
 (c) **Closing Documentation**.
  At such closing, the seller(s) shall deliver to the purchaser the certificate or certificates representing the Restricted Shares being purchased hereunder, duly endorsed for transfer, together with any other document or documents which may be reasonably required by the purchaser(s) to effectuate the transfer of title thereto, and the purchaser(s) shall deliver to the seller(s) the consideration therefor, as provided herein.

5.4. **Reduction for Indebtedness to Corporation**. *(For Redemption)*
 (a) Notwithstanding any other provision hereof, any amount which the Proposed Transferor or a deceased Stockholder's estate or Permitted Trust owes to the Corporation at the closing of a purchase of Restricted Shares, whether evidenced by a secured or unsecured loan, advance, receivable or otherwise, shall be satisfied by a direct reduction of the purchase price otherwise payable to such Proposed Transferor or such estate or Permitted Trust. Such reduction shall be taken from the first payment and all succeeding payments, in the order in which they otherwise would be made, in the amounts necessary to repay such loans, advances or receivables.
 (b) If the balance of such loan, advance or receivable exceeds the purchase price computed herein, then a promissory note shall be duly executed, dated and delivered to the purchaser by the Proposed Transferor or the Representative of the deceased Stockholder or the trustee of the Permitted Trust, as the case may be, on the closing date, in an original principal amount equal to the excess of the loan, advance or receivable over the Purchase Price. The note shall be on the terms and conditions set forth in Section 5.1 with respect to a Note for the installment payment of the Purchase Price for Restricted Shares.

5.5. **Restrictions on Corporate Actions During Repayment Period**. *(For Redemption)*
  Until the aggregate purchase price for said Restricted Shares is paid in full, except with the written consent of the seller, the Corporation shall not declare nor pay a dividend [except as provided in Section 11.5 hereof] unreasonably increase the rate of its officers' compensation, reorganize, recapitalize, merge or consolidate or, except in the ordinary course of its business, sell all or a substantial portion of its assets. So long as any part of the aggregate Purchase Price of the Restricted Shares being purchased hereunder remains unpaid, the seller shall have the right to enter the premises of the Corporation and there examine the books and records of the Corporation, alone or by

or with such attorneys or agents as the seller deems appropriate, the books and records of the Corporation, and shall have the right to receive, upon written request, copies of all accounting reports and tax returns prepared for or on behalf of the Corporation.

6. **Effect on Obligations**.

   6.1. **Release of Guaranties**. *(Optional)*

   In the event a deceased Stockholder had personally guaranteed any corporate obligation or had become a comaker on any corporate note, the Corporation and the surviving Stockholders shall take such steps as shall be reasonably necessary to relieve the Representative of such deceased Stockholder and the trustee of any Permitted Trust, as the case may be, from liability on any of said obligations or notes. If after a good faith effort, the Corporation and the surviving Stockholders are unable to so relieve the Representative of such deceased Stockholder or the trustee of such Permitted Trust from liability on any of said obligations or notes, the Corporation and the surviving Stockholders shall indemnify and hold the estate or Permitted Trust of the deceased Stockholder harmless from and against the payment of any of said obligations or notes.

   6.2. **No Effect On Corporate Obligations**.

   Nothing contained herein shall have any effect upon any amount due from the Corporation to a Proposed Transferor or a deceased Stockholder's estate or Permitted Trust at the closing of a purchase of Restricted Shares hereunder, whether evidenced by a secured or unsecured loan, advance, receivable or otherwise; such amount shall be repaid by the Corporation to the obligee thereof in accordance with its terms.

7. **Insurance**. *(Cross Purchase Alternative)*

   7.1. **Purchase of Insurance**.

   To fully or partially fund each Stockholder's obligation hereunder, each Stockholder has purchased or may purchase insurance policies insuring the life of each of the other Stockholders, naming such Stockholder as owner and revocable beneficiary thereof. The policies of insurance insuring the life of each Stockholder purchased by the other Stockholders hereunder are set out in Schedule A attached hereto, and by this reference made a part hereof.

   7.2. **Payment of Premiums**.

   Each Stockholder shall pay, or cause to be paid, within the grace period allowed, each premium due, or if applicable, the [planned periodic premium] (as such term is defined in such policy), on each policy of insurance purchased hereunder by the Stockholder, and shall, upon written request, give proof of payment of such premiums to the insured Stockholder, within thirty (30) days after the due date of each premium. If any Stockholder shall fail to pay any premium on any such policy as provided herein, the insured Stockholder shall have the right to terminate this Stockholders Agreement, as provided herein, or, at the Stockholder's option, may pay such premium and be reimbursed therefor, with interest at the Prime Rate, by such other Stockholder.

   7.3. **Ownership of Policies**.

   Each Stockholder shall be the owner of any such policy of insurance purchased by such Stockholder hereunder, and may exercise all incidents of ownership and other rights under any such policy (including, but not limited to, making or changing the allocation of the Policy Account (as such term is defined in the Policy) established pursuant to the terms of the Policy among the various investment options under the Policy, or selecting the death benefit option of the Policy), provided, however, that before exercising any such incident or right, such Stockholder shall give thirty (30) days written notice thereof to the insured Stockholder. The Stockholder owning any such policy shall have custody of such policy, and shall be named as revocable beneficiary thereof.

7.4. **Disposition of Policies Upon Sale of Shares or Termination of Agreement**.

(a) If any Stockholder sells or otherwise disposes of all of the Stockholder's Restricted Shares during the Stockholder's lifetime, or if this Stockholders Agreement is terminated for any reason, such Stockholder or each Stockholder, as the case may be, shall thereupon have the right to purchase any policy of insurance insuring the Stockholder's life owned by the other Stockholders, and upon the death of any Stockholder, the surviving Stockholders shall have the right to purchase any such policy insuring their respective lives from the executor or administrator of the estate of the deceased Stockholder. The purchase price, in each case, shall be the interpolated terminal reserve value of such policy, as of the date of such purchase, less any existing indebtedness against such policy, plus that portion of the premium on such policy paid prior to the date of such purchase which covers the period beyond the date of such purchase.

(b) The purchasing Stockholder shall exercise the purchase right granted the Stockholder herein within thirty (30) days after the event creating such purchase right, by written notice to the other Stockholders, or the Representative of any Stockholder, as the case may be, and by tendering the purchase price of such policy, in cash, to the selling Stockholder, or the Stockholder's Representative, as the case may be. The selling Stockholder, or the Stockholder's Representative, as the case may be, shall simultaneously deliver such policy to the insured Stockholder and shall execute and deliver to the insured Stockholder all documents reasonably required to transfer ownership of the policy to the insured Stockholder.

7.5. **Insurance Company Not a Party**.

No insurance company issuing any policy of insurance insuring the life of any Stockholder purchased hereunder shall be deemed a party to this Stockholders Agreement for any purpose, nor in any way responsible for its validity. No such insurance company shall be obligated to inquire as to the distribution of any proceeds payable by it under any policy issued on the life of any Stockholder purchased hereunder, and any such insurance company shall be fully discharged from any and all liability under the terms of any such policy, upon payment or other performance of its obligations in accordance with the terms of such policy.

8. **Insurance**. *(For Redemption)*

8.1. **Purchase of Insurance**.

To partially or fully fund its obligations hereunder, the Corporation has purchased or shall purchase insurance policies insuring the life of each of the Stockholders, naming itself as owner and revocable beneficiary thereof. The policies of insurance owned by the Corporation insuring the lives of the Stockholders are set out in Schedule A attached hereto, and by this reference made a part hereof.

8.2. **Payment of Premiums**.

The Corporation shall pay, within the grace period allowed, each premium due, or if applicable, the [planned periodic premium] (as such term is defined in such policy), on each policy owned by it insuring the lives of the Stockholders, and shall, upon written request, give proof of payment of such premiums to the insured Stockholder, within thirty (30) days after the due date of each premium. If the Corporation shall fail to pay any premium on such policy as provided herein, the insured Stockholder shall have the right to terminate this Stockholders Agreement as provided herein, or, at the Stockholder's option, may pay such premium and be reimbursed therefor, with interest at the Prime Rate, by the Corporation.

8.3. **Ownership of Policies**.

The Corporation shall be the owner of any such policy of insurance purchased by it hereunder, and may exercise all incidents of ownership and other rights under any such policy (including, but not limited to, making or changing the allocation of the Policy Account (as such term is defined in the Policy) established pursuant to the terms of the Policy among the various investment options under the Policy, or selecting the death benefit option of the Policy), provided, however, that before exercising any such incident or right, the Corporation shall give thirty (30) days written notice thereof to the insured Stockholder. The Corporation shall have custody of any such policy, and shall be named as revocable beneficiary thereof.

8.4. **Disposition of Policies Upon Sale of Shares or Termination of Agreement**.

(a) If any Stockholder sells or otherwise disposes of all of the Stockholder's Restricted Shares during the Stockholder's lifetime, or if this Stockholders Agreement is terminated for any reason, such Stockholder or each Stockholder, as the case may be, shall thereupon have the right to purchase any policy of insurance insuring the Stockholder's life owned by the Corporation. The purchase price shall be the interpolated terminal reserve value of such policy, as of the date of such purchase, less any existing indebtedness against such policy, plus that portion of the premium on such policy paid prior to the date of such purchase which covers the period beyond the date of such purchase.

(b) The purchasing Stockholder shall exercise the purchase right granted the Stockholder herein within thirty (30) days after the event creating such purchase right, by written notice to the Corporation and by tendering the purchase price of such policy, in cash, to the Corporation. The Corporation shall simultaneously deliver such policy to the insured Stockholder and shall execute and deliver to the insured Stockholder all documents reasonably required to transfer ownership of the policy to the insured Stockholder.

8.5. **Insurance Company Not a Party**.

No insurance company issuing any policy of insurance insuring the life of any Stockholder purchased hereunder shall be deemed a party to this Stockholders Agreement for any purpose, nor in any way responsible for its validity. No such insurance company shall be obligated to inquire as to the distribution of any proceeds payable by it under any policy issued on the life of any Stockholder purchased hereunder, and such insurance company shall be fully discharged from any and all liability under the terms of any such policy, upon payment or other performance of its obligations in accordance with the terms of such policy.

9. **Non-Competition**. *Optional*

During the continuation of the employment of any Stockholder who is an employee of the Corporation, and if any Stockholder who is an employee of the corporation ceases to be employed by the Corporation for any reason, for a period of twelve (12) months following the termination of employment of such Stockholder (regardless of whether the Corporation shall have exercised its option to purchase the Restricted Shares owned by such Stockholder as provided herein), no Stockholder will engage in any Competitive Activity that would directly harm the Corporation, without the prior written consent of the Corporation.

10. **Termination of Agreement**.

This Stockholders Agreement shall terminate upon the first to occur of any of the following events:

10.1. **Cessation of Business and Bankruptcy**.

The indefinite cessation of all active business by the Corporation, or the bankruptcy, receivership, or complete dissolution of the Corporation.

10.2. **At Election of Any Stockholder**. *(For Cross Purchase)*

(a) At the election of any Stockholder, exercisable upon written notice to the other Stockholders and the Corporation, if the Corporation or any other Stockholder violates any material provision of this Stockholders Agreement.

(b) At the election of any Stockholder on whose life insurance policies have been purchased by the other Stockholders to fund their obligations hereunder, if any other Stockholder fails to pay or cause to be paid premiums on the insurance policy owned by the Stockholder insuring the life of another Stockholder within the grace period thereof, and if such premium is not paid by the insured Stockholder in accordance herewith, and if such failure to pay causes the policy to lapse.

(c) At the election of any Stockholder on whose life insurance policies have been purchased by the other Stockholders to fund their obligations hereunder, if any other Stockholder assigns, surrenders, borrows against, changes the beneficiary of, elects to have the proceeds of any policy owned by the Stockholder on the life of such Stockholder paid other than in a lump sum, without the consent of the insured Stockholder.

10.3. **At Election of Any Stockholder**. *(For Redemption)*

(a) At the election of any Stockholder, exercisable by written notice to the other Stockholders and the Corporation, if the Corporation or any other Stockholder violates any material provision of this Stockholders Agreement

(b) At the election of any Stockholder on whose life insurance policies have been purchased by the Corporation to fund its obligations hereunder, if the Corporation fails to pay premiums on the insurance policy owned by it insuring the life of such Stockholder within the grace period thereof, and if such premium is not paid by the insured Stockholder in accordance herewith, and if such failure to pay causes the policy to lapse.

(c) At the election of any Stockholder on whose life insurance policies have been purchased by the Corporation to fund its obligations hereunder, if the Corporation assigns, surrenders, borrows against, changes the beneficiary of, elects to have the proceeds of any policy owned by it on the life of such Stockholder paid other than in a lump sum, without the consent of the insured Stockholder.

(d) Notwithstanding the foregoing, no Stockholder who is responsible for the payment of premiums described in Section 10.3(b) or for the exercise of incidents of ownership described in Section 10.3(c), by virtue of his position of employment or authority with the Corporation, may rely upon the failure of the Corporation to pay premiums or exercise incidents of ownership in a manner consistent with this Stockholders Agreement, to terminate this Stockholders Agreement pursuant to this Section 10.3.

10.4. **Upon Death of All Stockholders**. *(For Cross Purchase)*

The death of all of the Stockholders simultaneously or within a period of sixty (60) days; provided, however, that if this Stockholders Agreement shall terminate in accordance with the provisions of this paragraph, the respective Representatives of the estates of the Stockholders or the trustees of their Permitted Trusts, as the case may be, shall be entitled to collect the proceeds of the policies owned by their respective decedents, and to retain such proceeds free from the terms of this Stockholders Agreement;

10.5. **Upon Death of All Stockholders**. *(For Redemption)*

The death of all of the Stockholders simultaneously or within a period of sixty (60) days; provided, however, that if this Stockholders Agreement shall terminate in accordance with the provisions of this paragraph, the Corporation shall pay over and deliver to the respective Representatives of the estates of the Stockholders or the trustees of their Permitted Trusts, as the case may be, the proceeds of the policies owned by the Corporation insuring the lives of their respective decedents, who shall be entitled to retain such proceeds, free from the terms of this Stockholders Agreement;

10.6. **Acquisition of Shares by a Single Stockholder**.

The acquisition of all of the Restricted Shares by one Stockholder.

11. **S Corporation Status**. *(Optional)*

11.1. **Continuation of Status**.

(a)   If, at any time during the term hereof, the Corporation is an electing S Corporation, then it is expressly agreed by all of the parties hereto that, unless 100% of the holders of the Restricted Shares consent, the Corporation shall remain an S Corporation for federal income tax purposes, as defined in Subchapter S of Chapter 1 of Subtitle A of the Code, and that the provisions of this Section shall apply.

(b)   In pursuit of this intent, it is expressly agreed that no Stockholder shall sell, assign, hypothecate, transfer or pledge any interest in any Restricted Shares or do or cause or permit to be done any other act which would disqualify the Corporation from remaining an S Corporation. Each Stockholder represents and warrants that the Stockholder's ownership of the Restricted Shares shall not prevent the Corporation from making or maintaining its election to be treated as an S Corporation. It is further agreed that the Corporation and each of the Stockholders shall perform all acts within the time required, including, but not limited to, the execution of all documents, consents, elections, revocations and waivers necessary in order to maintain the status of the Corporation as an S Corporation.

11.2. **Agreement to Coordinate Estate Plans**.

Each of the Stockholders shall include in the Stockholder's Last Will and Testament and any Permitted Trust a direction to the Stockholder's Representative or Trustee, as the case may be, thereunder to comply herewith. It is expressly agreed that this provision shall apply to and be binding on the successors in interest of any deceased Stockholder, the Representative of any deceased Stockholder, and the Trustee of any Permitted Trust, as the case may be.

11.3. **Termination of Status as a Result of an Unpermitted Transfer**. *(Optional)*

If, as a result of any Stockholder's purported transfer of any of that Stockholder's Restricted Shares, or any interest therein, in a manner or to any Stockholder not specifically permitted by this Stockholders Agreement (whether by operation of law or by voluntary act or otherwise) the election by the Corporation to be treated as an S Corporation is terminated, that Stockholder shall pay to each of the other Stockholders in cash, on or before March 31 of each of the five years next following the year in which the purported transfer occurs, an amount which will reasonably compensate each other Stockholder for any loss or damage that the other Stockholder suffers as a result of the termination of the Corporation's election to be treated as an S Corporation. The amount of such compensation shall be calculated by the Corporation's regular certified public accountant, whose determination shall be binding and conclusive on all parties in interest.

11.4. **Effect of Termination of Status - Elections**.

If the Corporation's election to be treated as an S Corporation is terminated, or if a Stockholder's entire interest in the Corporation is terminated, then the Corporation shall make the election described by Sections 1362(e)(3) and 1377(a)(2) of the Code, respectively, and the Stockholders shall consent to such elections in the manner provided by the applicable federal income tax regulations.

Upon the determination of the Board of Directors that it is in the best interest of the Corporation's stockholders that the Corporation make the election described by Section 1368(e)(3) of the Code, the Corporation shall make such election, and the Stockholders shall consent to such election in the manner provided by the applicable federal income tax regulations.

11.5. **Required Distributions**.

(a) **Agreement to Vote Shares to Declare Dividends**.

The Stockholders hereby agree to vote their shares to cause the Corporation's Board of Directors to declare and then to cause the Corporation to pay with respect to any calendar year throughout which the Corporation's election to be treated as an S Corporation remains in effect dividend distributions on the shares in an amount at least equal to the amount set forth herein.

(b) **Amount of Required Dividend Distribution**.

Subject to any limitation imposed by applicable law, the amount of distribution which shall be paid hereunder shall equal the Corporation's taxable income for such year multiplied by the sum of the highest federal individual income tax bracket for the year plus the highest individual income tax bracket, if any, applicable to the State of _____ for the year.

(c) **Determination by Corporation's Regular Accountants**.

The Corporation's regular certified public accountants estimate of the Corporation's taxable income as of December 1 of each such year (annualized through yearend and taking into account any anticipated transactions not in the ordinary course of business or otherwise not properly reflected by annualized income) shall be final, conclusive, and binding upon the Corporation and all the Stockholders for purposes of determining the amount of dividend distributions that shall be made hereunder with respect to any such year.

(d) **Timing of Distributions**.

The Corporation shall make such distributions to the Stockholders (proportionately according to their respective ownership of shares) in full in cash on or before April 1st, September 1st and January 1st of the calendar quarter next following the year with respect to which the distributions are payable.

11.6. **Revocation of Election by Stockholder Consent**.

The Corporation's election to be treated as an S Corporation may be revoked under Section 1362(d) of the Code only upon the consent of holders of 100% of the Restricted Shares.

11.7. **Inadvertent Termination of Election**.

If any such election is inadvertently terminated under Section 1362(d)(2) or (d)(3) of the Code, then the Corporation immediately shall seek to obtain from the Internal Revenue Service a waiver of the termination of such election under Section 1362(f) of the Code and each Stockholder agrees to make such adjustments to the Stockholder's personal income tax return(s) as may be required by the Service to obtain the waiver. If the Service fails to grant the Corporation a waiver under Section 1362(f) of the Code, the Corporation shall request the Service's consent to refile an S election prior to the time specified in Section 1362(g) of the Code.

11.8. **Restrictions on Corporate Actions**.

So long as the Corporation's election to be treated as an S Corporation is in effect, the Corporation shall not take any action or engage in any transaction which would result in the termination of its election, including, but not limited to:

(a)   Any action or transaction resulting in the Corporation becoming an "ineligible corporation" under Section 1361(b)(2) of the Code;

(b)   The creation of a class of stock (other than nonvoting common capital stock) in addition to the Corporation's Restricted Shares of common capital stock; and

(c)   Borrowing funds from a Stockholder, unless all of the following conditions are met: (a) the loan is in writing and contains an unconditional promise to pay on demand or on a specific date; (b) the interest rate and payment dates are not contingent on profits, the discretion of the Corporation or other similar factors; and (c) the loan is not convertible into capital stock of the Corporation.

12. **Legend**.

During the continuance of this Stockholders Agreement, all certificates representing Restricted Shares, whether now or hereafter issued (including any voting trust certificate or similar instrument), shall be stamped with the following legend:

"This certificate and the transfer hereof are subject to that certain Stockholders Agreement dated _____, and it shall not be transferred upon the books of the Corporation unless the terms and conditions of said Stockholders Agreement have been fully complied with. A copy of said Stockholders Agreement is on file with the Secretary of the Corporation for the inspection and use of all of its Stockholders and all parties who may desire to purchase any of said shares."

13. **Definitions**.

For purposes of this Stockholders Agreement, the following terms shall have the meanings contained herein, unless the context requires otherwise:

13.1. **Adjusted Book Value**.

Whenever this Agreement specifies that a purchase shall be made at "Adjusted Book Value," this paragraph shall apply to such purchase.

The term "Adjusted Book Value" shall mean the book value of Restricted Shares, determined by the Corporation's regular certified public accountant, whose determination shall be final, binding and conclusive upon all parties in interest, and shall be made on a consolidated basis, if applicable, as of the end of the Corporation's most recent annual accounting period ended prior to the date of the event triggering the purchase and sale of Restricted Shares hereunder, with the following adjustments:

(a)   any dividend paid on said Restricted Shares after the date of the most recent financial statements for the Corporation (the "Statement Date") and prior to the date of a Notice of Proposed Transfer, which is not reflected as a liability thereon, shall be deducted therefrom;

(b)   any securities, real estate or other investments of the Corporation or any subsidiary thereof shall be valued at their fair market value on the Statement Date, as determined, in good faith, by the Board of Directors of the Corporation;

(c)   there shall be included as a liability, to the extent not otherwise reflected on the consolidated books of the Corporation, any income tax which would be due on the net unrealized appreciation on such investments, computed as if they had been sold for such fair market value on the Statement Date;

(d)   appropriate adjustment shall be made for all outstanding options or warrants to purchase capital stock of the Corporation and all securities convertible into capital stock of the Corporation, by computing said book value as if said options, warrants or securities had been fully exercised or converted, to the extent that such exercise or conversion would result in a lower book value;

(e)   in the case of a purchase of Restricted Shares at the death of a Stockholder, the excess of the proceeds of any life insurance policies owned by and payable to the Corporation insuring the life of such Stockholder at the Stockholder's death, over the cash surrender value of such policies on such date shall [shall not] be added thereto; and

(f)   after all other adjustments to book value provided herein have been made, interest shall be added at the Prime Rate per annum, from the Statement Date to the date of the closing of the purchase and sale of such Restricted Shares.

13.2.   **Agreed Value**. *(Alternative)*

Whenever this Agreement specifies that a purchase shall be made at "Agreed Value," this paragraph shall apply to such purchase.

(a)   The initial per share agreed value of the Restricted Shares shall be _____ Dollars per share, which shall be the per share agreed value for any Restricted Shares to be purchased hereunder, unless and until the same shall be changed by action of the Stockholders, as herein provided.

(b)   The Stockholders plan to agree among themselves, from time to time, and at least once each year, on the per share value of their Restricted Shares, which per share agreed value shall either be incorporated in a resolution adopted at the annual meeting of the stockholders of the Corporation and duly recorded in the signed minutes of said meeting, or shall be embodied in a written statement signed by all of the stockholders of the Corporation and filed with the secretary of the Corporation.

(c)   The purchase price per share to be paid for any Restricted Shares purchased hereunder shall be the latest agreed value per share, reduced by the amount of any dividend or dividends paid on said Restricted Shares after the date of determination of such value and prior to the date of such purchase, if any, and adjusted appropriately for any stock dividend, stock split, recapitalization, or other issuance by the Corporation of additional and outstanding shares of its common stock occurring after the last determination of such value.

(d) If more than eighteen months (18) but no more than thirty-six months (36), have elapsed between the latest determination of the per share agreed value of the Restricted Shares, then the price per share to be paid for any Restricted Shares purchased based upon the Agreed Value shall be increased or decreased by an amount equal to the increase or decrease in the per share Adjusted Book Value thereof, from the date of the last determination of the per share Agreed Value thereof to the end of the Corporation's most recent accounting period ending prior to the event giving rise to the sale of the Restricted Shares.

(e) If the Agreed Value is in effect for more than thirty-six months (36), then the Agreed Value, including any adjustments made in accordance with Section 13.2(d), shall be deemed void, and the Agreed Value shall be the Appraised Value as determined in accordance with Section 13.3.

13.3. **Appraised Value**. *(Alternative)*

Whenever this Agreement specifies that a purchase shall be made at "Appraised Value," this paragraph shall apply to such purchase.

The term "Appraised Value" shall mean the per share value to be paid for any Restricted Shares purchased hereunder, which shall be determined by appraisal in the following manner:

(a) The per share value of the Corporation's Restricted Shares shall be determined by a qualified appraiser selected by the Corporation, at the Corporation's expense, within forty-five (45) days from the date of an event triggering the purchase of Restricted Shares hereunder.

(b) The Corporation shall distribute copies of the appraisal to the parties hereto upon receipt.

(c) In the event that a party to the sale of any Restricted Shares does not agree with the price per share determined by the Corporation's appraiser (the "Disputing Party"), then the Disputing Party must give written notice that the Disputing Party does not agree with the value of the Restricted Shares as determined by the Corporation's appraiser to the Stockholders and the Corporation within thirty (30) days of the purchaser's receipt of the Corporation's appraisal. The Disputing Party may retain an independent qualified appraiser, at the Disputing Party's expense, to determine the Appraisal Value per share within thirty (30) days of receipt of the Corporation's appraisal. For purposes hereof, a member of either the American Society of Appraisers or the Appraisal Institute shall be considered a qualified appraiser.

(d) In the event the valuation of the Disputing Party's appraiser differs from the valuation of the Corporation's appraiser by less than ten percent (10%), then the average of the two valuations shall be the Appraisal Value. In the event the valuation of the Disputing Party's appraiser differs from the valuation of the Corporation's appraiser by more than ten percent (10%), then the Corporation's appraiser and the Disputing Party's appraiser shall jointly select, within thirty (30) days of the Disputing Party's appraisal, a third independent qualified appraiser, at both parties' expense (share equally), to determine the per share value of the stock, in which case, this third valuation shall be the Appraisal Value.

13.4. **Code**.

The term "Code" shall mean the Internal Revenue Code of 1986, as amended.

13.5. **Competitive Activity**. [Optional]

The term "Competitive Activity" shall mean engaging in any of the following activities: (i) directly or indirectly soliciting, diverting, taking away, appropriating or otherwise interfering with any of the employees, customers or suppliers of the Corporation's business, or (ii) employment by (including serving as a director or an officer of), or providing consulting services to, any company that is in direct competition with the Corporation, or any affiliate or subsidiary of such company, at the time this Stockholders Agreement is terminated (each, a "Direct Competitor"), or (iii) owning equity or debt interests in a Direct Competitor; or (iv) actively participating in the management of a Direct Competitor.

13.6. **Disability**.

The term "Disability" shall mean a Stockholder's inability to perform the duties of the Stockholder's position with the Corporation because of a physical or mental impairment which can reasonably be expected to be of presumably permanent, long, continued or indefinite duration, as determined by a competent professional medical practitioner selected by the Stockholder, which selection shall be subject to the reasonable approval of the Corporation. In the event the Stockholder and the Corporation are unable to agree upon the selection of such a practitioner, each shall select such a practitioner who, if they are unable to agree with respect to the Stockholder's disability, shall select a third such practitioner; the determination of a majority of such practitioners shall be final, binding and conclusive upon all parties in interest.

13.7. **Donee**. *(Optional)*

The term "Donee" or "Donees" shall mean, as to any Stockholder: (i) the transferring Stockholder's spouse or any of the descendants of such Stockholder; (ii) a trust, whether revocable or irrevocable established for the benefit of the transferring Stockholder, such Stockholder's spouse or the descendants of such Stockholder, which is not a Permitted Trust; (iii) a limited partnership whose only partners are the transferring Stockholder, such Stockholder's spouse, the descendants of such Stockholder, a revocable trust created by such Stockholder or such Stockholder's spouse and/or descendants, or an irrevocable trust solely for the benefit of such Stockholder or such Stockholder's spouse and/or descendants, or (iv) a limited liability company whose only Members are the transferring Stockholder, such Stockholder's spouse, the descendants of such Stockholder, a revocable trust created by such Stockholder or such Stockholder's spouse and/or descendants, or an irrevocable trust solely for the benefit of such Stockholder or such Stockholder's spouse and/or descendants.

13.8. **Notice of Proposed Transfer**.

The term "Notice of Proposed Transfer" shall mean the written notice required to be given hereunder by a Stockholder to the Corporation and to each other Stockholder, indicating that the Stockholder giving such notice intends to transfer or dispose of the Stockholder's Restricted Shares

13.9. **Permitted Trust**.

The term "Permitted Trust" shall mean a wholly revocable trust created by a Stockholder for the Stockholder's benefit during the Stockholder's lifetime, as to which, at the time of a transfer of Restricted Shares to such trust, the Stockholder is either the sole Trustee or a co-Trustee.

13.10. **Prime Rate**.

The term "Prime Rate" shall mean the annual interest rate which the Corporation's primary commercial bank quotes as of the closing date of any purchase and sale transaction provided for herein as its "prime" or "base" rate, provided, that if at such time the Corporation does not have a primary commercial bank, then such term shall mean such rate of _____, as of such date. Notwithstanding the foregoing, in no event shall the Prime Rate be less than the lowest rate of interest required in order to avoid imputation of interest at any higher rate for federal income tax purposes under the unstated interest, original issue discount or belowmarket loan provisions of the Internal Revenue Code of 1986, as amended, or any similar provision as may be applicable to said transaction.

13.11. **Proposed Transferor**.

The term "Proposed Transferor" shall mean the Stockholder giving a Notice of Proposed Transfer to both the Corporation and each other Stockholder.

13.12. **Ratable Option**.

The term "Ratable Option" shall mean an option to purchase a number of Restricted Shares equal to the total number of Restricted Shares being offered for sale multiplied by a fraction, the numerator of which is the number of Restricted Shares owned by the Stockholder possessing such option and the denominator of which is the total number of Restricted Shares owned by all Stockholders possessing such option.

13.13. **Representative**.

The term "Representative" shall mean the executor, administrator, personal representative or other legal representative of a Stockholder's probate estate, as the context requires.

13.14. **Restricted Shares**.

The term "Restricted Shares" shall mean shares of capital stock of the Corporation now or hereafter owned or acquired by any Stockholder, and all other shares of such capital stock which may, from time to time, be issued in respect of any such shares, including, without limitation, all shares issued as a stock dividend or stock split, or pursuant of any plan of reorganization, recapitalization, merger, consolidation, or otherwise.

13.15. **Stockholder**.

The term "Stockholder" or "Stockholders" shall mean the Stockholder parties to this Stockholders Agreement and any additional stockholders who become stockholders of the Corporation hereafter, by purchase, for value, or by other acquisition, whether or not described in Section 2.1. [Such term shall specifically not include the Donee or Donees of a Stockholder].

14. **Miscellaneous Provisions**.

14.1. **Agreement Enforceable.**

The parties hereto acknowledge and agree that each Stockholder will receive substantial and valuable benefits under the covenants and agreements set forth herein, and that the Corporation and each Stockholder would not have executed and delivered this Agreement, if the other Stockholders had not entered into the covenants and agreements set forth herein. Accordingly, the parties intend that such agreements and covenants be enforceable and that it would be inequitable if a court or judicial tribunal were to not enforce such covenants and agreements to the fullest extent provided herein.

14.2. **Specific Performance**.

The capital stock of the Corporation cannot be readily purchased or sold in the open market, and, for that reason, among others, the parties hereto will be irreparably damaged in the event that this Stockholders Agreement is not specifically enforced. Should any dispute arise concerning the transfer or other disposition of any Restricted Shares, an injunction may be issued restraining any proposed transfer or disposition, pending the determination of such controversy. In the event of any controversy concerning the purchase or sale or other transfer of any Restricted Shares pursuant to the provisions of this Stockholders Agreement, the same shall be enforceable in a court of equity, by a decree of specific performance, provided, however, that such remedy shall be cumulative and not exclusive, and shall be in addition to any other remedy or remedies which any of the parties hereto may have.

14.3. **Violation of Agreement**.

(a)   No attempted transfer or disposition of Restricted Shares otherwise than in compliance with the terms of this Stockholders Agreement shall be effective; any such attempted transfer or disposition shall be void ab initio. No certificate representing Restricted Shares shall be transferred on the books of the Corporation without a written determination from the Corporations regular corporate counsel that such transfer complies with all material terms hereof.

(b)   No alleged transferee of Restricted Shares who shall receive any Restricted Shares otherwise than in compliance with the provisions of this Stockholders Agreement shall be entitled to have such Restricted Shares transferred to the Stockholder on the books of the Corporation, nor to have vested in the Stockholder any rights with respect to voting, dividends or other rights in such Restricted Shares, and all such Restricted Shares shall remain subject to all of the provisions hereof.

(c)   In the event that any Stockholder, the Representative of the Stockholder's estate or the trustee of any Permitted Trust [or Donee], as the case may be, shall fail to tender certificates representing any Restricted Shares purchased hereunder at the closing thereof, such certificate shall no longer be deemed outstanding after the date set herein for such closing, and all rights with respect to such Restricted Shares shall forthwith cease and terminate, excepting only the right of the Stockholder or the Stockholder's Representative or trustee [or Donee], as the case may be, to receive the purchase price therefor from the purchaser thereof, upon surrender of such certificates.

14.4. **Notices**.

Any notice, offer or demand required or permitted to be given under the provisions of this Stockholders Agreement by one party to another shall be in writing, and shall be signed by the party giving or making the same, and may be given either by delivering the same to such other party personally, or by mailing the same by United States certified mail, postage prepaid, return receipt requested, to such other party addressed to the Stockholder's or its last known address as shown on the records of the Corporation. The date of such mailing shall be deemed the date of such mailed notice, offer or demand.

14.5. **Execution**.

This Stockholders Agreement shall be executed in multiple original counterparts, each of the Stockholders to receive one of said multiple original copies, and one of said multiple original copies to be filed in the minute book of the Corporation, by its Secretary, each of which counterparts shall be deemed an original, but all of which shall constitute one and the same Stockholders Agreement.

14.6. **Amendment**.

Any amendment to or cancellation of the terms, conditions and provisions of this Stockholders Agreement shall be made in writing, and shall be signed by all of the parties hereto, their successors, assigns or legal representatives.

14.7. **<u>Binding Effect</u>**.

This Stockholders Agreement, and any amendment hereto made as provided herein, shall be binding upon and inure to the benefit of the Corporation and its successors and assigns, and the Stockholders, their [Donees], heirs, Representatives and trustees of any Permitted Trusts and their respective successors.

14.8. **<u>Conflict With Articles Or By-Laws</u>**.

It is expressly agreed that whether or not the Articles or By-Laws of the Corporation fully incorporate the provisions hereof, or any of them, the parties' rights and obligations with respect to their Restricted Shares shall be governed by this Stockholders Agreement, which shall prevail in the event of any ambiguity or inconsistency between this Stockholders Agreement and such Articles or By-Laws.

14.9. **<u>Governing Law</u>**.

This Stockholders Agreement shall be governed by and construed under the laws of the State of [_____], without regard to its conflict of law rules.

IN WITNESS WHEREOF, the Stockholders have executed this Stockholders Agreement, and the Corporation has caused this Stockholders Agreement to be executed on its behalf, in multiple original counterparts, as of the day and year first above written.

<<CORPORATION NAME>>

By_____

Name:
Title:

"CORPORATION"

_____
Stockholder1

_____
Stockholder2

_____
Stockholder3

"STOCKHOLDERS"

Index